Grammar ❷
Games and Activities

Grammar 2
Games and Activities

Deirdre Howard-Williams

To the memory of Kirsten Doizelet,
fellow teacher and friend

Series Editor
Peter Watcyn-Jones

PENGUIN ENGLISH

Pearson Education Limited
Edinburgh Gate
Harlow
Essex CM20 2JE, England
and Associated Companies throughout the world.

ISBN 978-0-582-46564-0

First published 2001

9 10 8

Every effort has been made to trace the copyright holders in every case. The publishers would be
interested to hear from any not acknowledged here.

Designed and typesetting by Ferdinand Pageworks, London
Illustrations by Rupert Besley and Ross Thomson
Printed in China.   SWTC/08

Acknowledgements
The publishers make grateful acknowledgement for permission to reproduce the following
photographs:
p 80, woman leaning head on hand, © EyeWire, Inc.; p 80, three photographs with women
looking at the camera, © Digital Vision Ltd; p 81 and p 119, © Digital Vision Ltd.

Published by Pearson Education Limited in association with Penguin Books Ltd, both
companies being subsidiaries of Pearson plc.

For a complete list of the titles available from Penguin English please visit our website at
www.penguinenglish.com, or write to your local Pearson Education office or to: Penguin English
Marketing Department, Pearson Education, Edinburgh Gate, Harlow, Essex CM20 2JE.

Contents

Key to contents table

Activity type		Preparation	
🧍	individual	📄	1 handout to copy
🧍🧍	pair work	📄📄	several handouts to copy
🧍🧍🧍	group work	✂️📄	1 handout to copy and cut up
🧍🧍🧍🧍	whole class activity	✂️📄📄	several handouts to copy and cut up
🎓	teacher-led activity	✂️📄	handout to be cut up into several pieces or into cards

	Game/Activity	Time	Grammar/Topic	Activity type	Preparation	Pages
Beginner/Elementary						
1	Do you agree with me?	20–25 mins	Present simple; agreeing and disagreeing	🧍🧍🧍🧍	📄	1/47
2	Words and stories	20–25 mins	Word order; time markers; punctuation	🧍🧍🧍	✂️📄	1/48
3	Questions and answers	30 mins	Question words; past and present tenses; asking for information; expressing certainty and opinions	🧍🧍🧍	📄	2/49
4	When's your birthday?	20 mins	Dates; giving information	🧍🧍🧍🧍	✂️📄	3/50
5	Descriptions	15–20 mins	Present simple; present continuous; *There is/are*; prepositions	🧍🧍	📄📄	3/51–52
6	Correct the mistakes	25–30 mins	Revision of elementary grammar points	🧍🧍	📄	4/53
7	Crosswords – Write your own clues	30 mins	Irregular past tense	🧍 🧍🧍	✂️📄📄	5/54–56
8	Saying numbers	20 mins	Numbers	🧍🧍	✂️📄	5/57
9	Great Britain quiz	15–20 mins	Asking questions; giving information	🧍🧍🧍	✂️📄	6/58
10	Can you remember?	20 mins	Present continuous; *There is/are*; question words	🧍🧍	📄📄	7/59–60
11	Two letters	20 mins	Apostrophes; spelling; letter writing; formal vs informal style	🧍 🧍🧍	✂️📄	7/61
12	Me and my snake	25–30 mins	Present simple; discourse markers	🧍🧍🧍	✂️📄	8/62–63

Game/Activity	Time	Grammar/Topic	Activity type	Preparation	Pages

Introduction

Grammar Games and Activities 2 forms part of the Penguin series of resource books for teachers. This book can be used independently of Book 1 and provides teachers with 60 completely new and up-to-the-minute activities for practising and revising grammar. These activities range in level from elementary to advanced and include a wide variety of types: ranking activities, crosswords, talking about photographs, quizzes, making comparisons, correcting mistakes, giving your opinion, etc.

Each activity contains material to be photocopied, usually one or two sheets, and clear step-by-step instructions to the teacher on preparation and organisation. **Grammar Games and Activities 2** can be used with adults and teenagers at all levels and in different classes to give extra practice in grammar in a fun and stimulating way.

The grammar items in the book have been carefully chosen to cover a wide base with the emphasis on the most frequently encountered e.g. asking and answering questions in various tenses. Each activity is centred on one specific grammar point which is clearly explained with examples in the Teacher's Notes and most will additionally practise supplementary grammar points, which are also presented in detail.

Most of the activities will involve the students working in pairs or in small groups, which is an excellent way of making the learning process more dynamic and enjoyable. Students will see that grammar is a necessary part of communication and can be fun!

The organisation of this book

Grammar Games and Activities 2 has been organised by level. There are five levels:

1   Beginner/Elementary
2   Elementary/Pre-intermediate
3   Pre-intermediate/Intermediate
4   Intermediate/Upper Intermediate
5   Upper Intermediate/Advanced

with twelve activities in each level.

However, classes vary enormously and these levels are only a guide, since the games in this book practise and reinforce vital grammar items which can be useful to everyone.

Classroom organisation

The activities in **Grammar Games and Activities 2** are sufficiently flexible to be done in classes of all sizes and extra suggestions are made for very large numbers.

Grammar point

The detailed contents list will show at a glance the grammar point that is being practised in each game so this is the first place to look if you wish to find a game to either present or revise a specific grammar point with your class.

Some grammar points are dealt with in several different games so you can go back to the book a few lessons later and find another activity to use for reinforcement.

Time

There is an indication in the contents list and also in the Teacher's Notes as to the approximate time each activity will take. This will of course vary from class to class and will depend on how thoroughly you wish to exploit the activity. However it does give an indication and can help you decide if you wish to make the game the main focus of the lesson or use it either at the beginning (as an ice-breaker and introduction) or at the end of the lesson (as a relaxation and revision).

Preparing the activity before class

The Teacher's Notes to each activity have a special section: Preparation.
This section tells you exactly what you need to do before the class starts i.e., how many pages to photocopy, how many copies are needed and if the copies need to be cut up in any way.

Introducing the activity

The Teacher's Notes start with suggestions on how to introduce each activity. It may often be useful to revise the grammar point first and write some examples up for students to refer to while the game is going on. These can be wiped off once the game has got started and students start to use the structures automatically.

Always explain very clearly what to do and it is often a good idea to do an example yourself with one of the students.

For most of the activities it is a good idea to set a time-limit and write this up so that everyone can see it. Give a warning shortly before it expires so that students can start to finish off. It may be that some students have not finished but it is inevitable that people will finish at different times and it may be a better idea to play the game a second time.

Pair work and group work

There are various types of activities: some where students work individually, some where they work in pairs and some where they cooperate in small groups.

Where possible, rearrange the classroom slightly to make it easier for students to work in pairs or groups without disturbing others. Where this is not possible, students doing pair work should work with the person sitting beside them or the person in front or behind (they just need to turn round). For group work, two students can easily turn their chairs round to face two others behind them. When you have an uneven number of students, most pair activities can be done by three people (if necessary, two students against one).

As far as possible, vary the pairs and groups so that students do not always work with the same people. It can sometimes be useful to mix stronger and weaker students in a small group so that they can help one another.

The enormous advantage of working in pairs and groups is that it gives everyone a chance to speak in a non-threatening environment, i.e. with a fellow-student and not in front of the teacher and the whole class. Students will learn from each other in a natural way that approximates more to the world outside and gets away from some of the constraints of the classroom. If this type of activity is new to them, it is useful to explain its advantages and to encourage them to take full advantage by participating as much as they can and sticking strictly to English!

The role of the teacher while this is going on is to facilitate communication by walking round the classroom, pausing briefly beside each pair/group. If all is going well, just encourage and move on. If things are not going so well, offer help and encouragement as needed to get students working well together.

While walking round, it is useful to have a small notebook or piece of paper on which you note down any persistent mistakes you hear or common problems. You can discuss these with the whole class during the feedback session – it is usually better to avoid saying who made each mistake as this can have a discouraging effect!

Feedback session and follow-up work

Each activity should end with a feedback session for the whole class.

The Teacher's Notes contain detailed suggestions on how to conduct this session for each individual activity. This checking and evaluation is an integral part of the activity and it is important to leave enough time for it.

Teachers may like to extend the activity into some kind of written follow-up work to reinforce what has been practised in class and most of the games have ideas for further activities and for homework.

A note about photocopying

Since this is a photocopiable book with each activity containing one or more handouts, it may be worth looking at ways of reducing the costs – both in terms of time and money. The material to be photocopied can be divided into two types: (a) handouts which the students write on, and (b) material which the students use but do not write on. Of the latter, many are cut into cards.

For material that can be re-used, wherever possible try mounting them on cards and protecting them either by laminating them or (a cheaper solution) by keeping them in clear plastic folders. The extra initial effort will certainly pay off as subsequent photocopying costs and time will be reduced greatly.

Part 1: **Teacher's notes**

Beginner/Elementary

1   Do you agree with me?

Time: 20–25 minutes
Activity type: Whole class mingle; ice-breaker
Preparation: Make one copy of page 47 for
                   each student

Grammar points
Making statements in the present simple tense:
My favourite colour is red. I like going out with my friends.
Asking others for their opinions
What about you? Do you agree? What's your favourite ...?
Agreeing
I agree. My favourite colour's green too.
Disagreeing
No, I don't agree. My favourite is ... .

Method

1   Give each student a copy of the handout and go through the statements, explaining vocabulary where necessary and giving students time to work individually to underline their favourite items each time.

2   Explain that they are now going to try to find five other people in the class who agree with them by asking questions and noting down the names of those who agree in the second column.

3   Write on the board an example of what they should say: *My favourite colour is yellow./I like yellow.* followed by *What about you?/Do you agree?/What's your favourite colour?* Then discuss ways of agreeing: *Yes, I agree./I agree with you./It's my favourite too.* and ways of disagreeing: *No, I don't agree./My favourite is ... .* Practise with one or two students as an example.

4   Now give fifteen minutes for students to circulate and ask one another the questions. While they are doing this, circulate yourself to check they are using the constructions correctly and that everyone is participating and noting down

names. Stop the activity after fifteen minutes and ask everyone to sit down.

5   Do a whole class feedback, asking who found five people to agree with them on each topic and who didn't. You might like to find out which were the most popular answers for a class profile e.g., *In this class we like cats, the colour yellow and playing games in English.*, etc. It might also be interesting for students to say who in the class agreed with them.

6   A follow-on activity could be to ask students to work in groups to make up their own questionnaires.

2   Words and stories

Time: 20–25 minutes
Activity type: Group work; building up a story
Preparation: Make one copy of page 48 for
                   each group of 4–6 students
                   Cut up into 75 pieces (some of
                   which are blank)

Grammar points
Word order of the English sentence
Aishling stood by the window and thought about her brother who was coming home for Christmas.
Time markers
first/then/during/just then
Punctuation
full stops/capital letters/setting out of direct speech

Method

1   Divide the class up into small groups (4–6 students) and ask them to sit round a table. Give each group a full set of the 62 words and 13 blank cards, shuffled. The story is in the correct order on page 48.

2   Explain that the words form the beginning of a story and their task is to work together to reconstruct this story. Give them the first word: 'During' and point out that the punctuation and capital letters will help.

3   Students now work in their groups to reconstruct the story using all the words. Circulate to give help and encouragement where needed.

4 When a group feel they have constructed the story they should ask you to check it. Once it is correct they can start the second part of the activity. When most groups have finished, bring this first part to an end and check the story.

5 For the second part of the activity, the students work to write a new sentence to follow on from the final sentence with a maximum of thirteen words. They should talk about this first and write it in rough for you to check. Then they write the words on the blank cards and shuffle them.

6 Collect these cards in and redistribute to different groups. Give them time to reconstruct the sentence and then write the different sentences on the board. You might like to discuss which are the most effective.

7 For follow-up work, ask students to continue the story for homework.

3 Questions and answers

Time: 30 minutes
Activity type: Quiz; communicative activity for small groups
Preparation: Make one copy of page 49 for each small group of 3–5 students

Grammar points
Question words
who/what/why/where/how much/how many, etc.
Past and present tenses
A spider has …/The colours are …
The Titanic sank …/Man walked on the Moon …
Asking for information
Do you know …:?
Expressing certainty and opinions
I know …/I'm sure …/I don't think so …/I've no idea.
Offering information using the first conditional
We'll tell you … if you tell us …

Method

1 Divide the class up into small groups (3–5 students) and tell them you are going to test their general knowledge as well as their English knowledge! Give each group a copy of the handout.

2 Firstly they look at the questions and put in the correct question word. You may like to revise possible words on the board first if you feel your class needs this. Circulate to give help and encouragement.

3 When a group have finished the question words, they should ask you to check their work before they go on to the answers. Encourage them to talk among themselves to find the answers, using *Do you know?* and answering *I know …/I think …/I'm not sure/I've got no idea.*, etc.

4 Once most groups have finished and found as many answers as they can, tell them they can ask other groups and trade answers. They need to say what they need to know and offer to trade something the other group needs. Write some useful expressions on the board, such as *We don't know …, do you? If you tell us …, we'll tell you … .*

5 Leave about five minutes for this interchange and then stop the activity. Ask different students to ask and answer questions and congratulate the group who got the most right answers. If you like, you can take in the answers and distribute them to other groups to correct.

6 For a follow-up activity, ask groups to write two or three more questions (to which they must know the answers). Then see if any group is able to beat the whole class by asking a question nobody else can answer!

Key

1 Who – An American film star **2** What – William **3** Which – Lithuania **4** How many – 100 **5** Where – Nepal and China **6** Who – Bill Gates **7** When – 1969 **8** Whose – Charles, Anne, Andrew, Edward **9** Why – It's a symbol of the union of England, Wales, Scotland and Northern Ireland **10** What – Red, white and blue **11** When – 26th December **12** How many – 9 **13** When – 1912 **14** Which – Yen **15** How much – £44

4 When's your birthday?

Time:	20 minutes
Activity type:	Whole class mingle asking and answering questions
Preparation:	Make one copy of page 50 per pair of students and cut it in half

Grammar points
Dates
14th September/23rd June/1st March 1947, etc.
Asking about birthdays
When's your birthday?
Giving information
It's on ...
Two people have birthdays in May. Nobody has a birthday on the 30th. etc.

Method

1 Start by introducing the idea of birthdays – you might like to say when yours is or ask the class to guess (date only and not year!). Revise months of year and use of ordinal numbers (1st/5th etc.) for dates.

2 Divide the class into two groups, A and B, and give each student the appropriate half of the handout. Explain that they are going to ask everyone in the group when their birthday is. Practise the question *When's your birthday?* and the answer *It's on ...* if necessary for your class. First, however, they are going to estimate what answers they will receive and how many people will have birthdays in the months and on the exact dates on their sheets. Leave a few minutes for them to think about this and write their individual estimates in the appropriate columns.

3 Now give time for a whole class mingle where everyone asks everyone else and notes down the appropriate information on their sheets.

4 When this has been done by the majority of the class, stop the activity and put students into small groups. They check that what they have is the same (it should be!) and write a few sentences to sum up what they have discovered. Write some

structures on the board for guidelines, e.g. *Three people have birthdays in March. Nobody has a birthday on the 8th.*, etc.

5 For whole class feedback, ask who estimated correctly and then ask them to tell the class that information first.

6 Practising the years people are born can be too personal so is best done with celebrities. Write two names on the board: Arnold Schwarzeneggar and Prince William and ask everyone to write down their full date of birth (a guess). Explain the difference between *birthday* and *date of birth* and practise how to say years. Then see if anyone guessed – or knew – either of the dates of birth and if not, who came nearest.

Key

Arnold Schwarzeneggar–30/7/47;
Prince William–21/6/82

7 This activity can be prolonged for further practise by asking students to think of or find out about the dates of birth of other famous people and then ask others in the class.

5 Descriptions

Time:	15–20 minutes
Activity type:	Pair work
Preparation:	Make copies of pages 51 and 52 per student

Grammar points
Present simple used in descriptions
She has long hair.
Negatives
Her clothes aren't smart./The room's not tidy.
has got
She's got short hair.
Present continuous
She's smiling.
There is .../There are ...
There is a bed./There are posters.
Prepositions
There's a book on the bed.

Method

1 Give everyone a copy of handout A. If you think it necessary, spend a few minutes

3

eliciting some vocabulary about the drawings and write this up on the board. This is to help students in the next part when they talk about the drawings.

2   Divide the class into pairs, A and B, and explain that the object of the activity is to give clear descriptions and to listen carefully. Briefly revise *She has .../She's got .../She hasn't got .../She's ...ing* before starting. Students sit back to back and Student A starts by describing three of the four pictures of the girls to Student B. Allow two minutes for this. Student B just listens. When the two minutes is up, shout 'stop'. Both students then write down the number of the photo that was not described. Then you say 'show' and they compare what they have written. Congratulate those who were correct and ask the others why they thought otherwise.

3   Give everyone a copy of handout B. Now it is Student B's turn to describe three of the four photos of the girls' rooms. Briefly revise: *There is .../There are .../There isn't .../There aren't ...* and a few prepositions: *on/under/beside,* etc. Proceed as above and once again congratulate those who got it right.

4   As a quick final activity, you could give the class one of the pictures and see how many sentences they can generate to describe it.

5   For homework, they could choose one of the photos and write a short description.

6   Correct the mistakes

Time: 25–30 minutes
Activity type: Pair work (or can be done in small groups)
Preparation: Make one copy of page 53 per pair of students (or if you feel it would be useful for students to keep a copy for reference, make one copy per student)

Grammar points
Revision of basic elementary grammar points
Singular/plural

There is/There are
Tags
isn't he?
Verbs followed by gerund
enjoy watching
Superlatives
most beautiful/prettiest
would like followed by infinitive
I would like to go
Adjectives and adverbs
good/well
Present perfect continuous
How long have you been ...?
s on third person singular
She wants
Verbs not normally used in the continuous
I understand.
Use of present continuous
He's reading.
Countable and uncountable
How much/How many
Use of past tense with *born*
I/He/She was born ...

Method

1   Divide the class into pairs (or groups of 2–4). Give each pair a copy of the handout and explain that they are going to do an activity based on their knowledge of grammar. They need to read each sentence and decide if it is correct or not. If it is correct, they write 'right' in the second column and continue. If it is incorrect, they write 'wrong' in the column and then correct the mistake in the third column.

2   Give ten minutes for this, circulating to give help and encouragement where necessary.

3   Stop the game after ten minutes and take in all the sheets (after asking pairs to write their names on). Redistribute to others and start to check. Ask different students to say if the sentences are right or not and to make the necessary corrections.

4   Markers should give one point for correctly identifying right or wrong sentences and then a further point for making the correction. Any wrong identifications or corrections lose a mark and should be written as minus marks in the final column.

5   Finally the scores are added up and returned to the original pairs. Find out who are the grammar champions and congratulate them.

6   If certain grammar points caused problems, you might like to do a game on these for reinforcement. Look at the contents list to this book or *Grammar Games and Activities 1*.

Key

1 Wrong – *is* should be *are* **2** Right **3** Right **4** Wrong – *most pretty* should be *prettiest* **5** Wrong – *would like go* should be *would like to go* **6** Wrong – *so good* should be *so well* **7** Right **8** Wrong – *want* should be *wants* **9** Wrong – *reads* should be *is reading* **10** Wrong – *How much* should be *How many* **11** Wrong – *I am understanding* should be *I understand* **12** Right

7   Crosswords – Write your own clues

Time: 30 minutes
Activity type: Working individually and then in pairs; writing clues and filling in a crossword
Preparation: Make enough copies for half the class of page 54 (Student A), page 55 (Student B) and page 56 (answer sheet)
                 Cut the answer sheet into two parts

Grammar points
Irregular past tenses of the most common verbs
spoke/was/took/made, etc.
Using verbs in simple contexts
She made a cake for tea./The sun shone all day., etc.

Method

1   Divide the class into pairs (A and B) and give each one the appropriate handouts (blank crossword and answers).

2   Explain that they are going to write the clues to their crossword so that it can later be given to their partner to complete (they leave the grid blank and must not show the answer sheet to their partner). All the words in the crosswords are irregular past tenses of common English verbs as they will see by

looking at the answers. They need to give clear clues, using words or pictures. They must not give the infinitive or present of the verb, but should give a context and a blank to show how the word is used.

3   Do the first clue in each crossword as an example. Crossword A 1 down – the answer is *made* so the clue could be: *She ... a cake for the party.*

Crossword B 1 down – the answer is *took* so the clue could be: *She ... her coat off and sat down.*

4   Give ten minutes for students to write clues, circulating to give help where needed. Anyone who finds it difficult could work with another student with the same crossword.

5   Now students exchange crosswords with their partner and have another ten minutes to complete their crosswords. If they have difficulties, they can use a dictionary.

6   The winners are the pair who both manage to complete their crosswords correctly in the shortest time. Students can check their work by using the answer sheet.

8   Saying numbers

Time: 20 minutes
Activity type: Pair work
Preparation: Make one copy of page 57 per pair of students and cut in half

Grammar points
Numbers and how to say them
Figures
one thousand, three hundred and four
Fractions
one third/two fifths
Decimals
two point seven five
Scores
Wolverhampton three; Leeds nil
Calculations
seven plus three equals ten
Kings and Queens
George the fourth
Temperature
twenty degrees/minus ten degrees

Method

1 Divide the class into pairs, A and B, and give each student the relevant section of the handout. Students should sit back to back or in some way so that they cannot see what their partner is writing.

2 Now they take it in turns to read out what they have in each category to each other and they note it down in the blank column. This will continue until the list is finished (there are twenty items in each list).

3 Now stop the activity and ask students to compare what they have written with what is on their partner's sheet. They should talk together about the correct way to say the numbers. During this time, circulate to note which items have caused problems. Ask pairs to give you their combined scores (out of 40) and congratulate the class champions.

4 Finish with a whole class round-up where you go through the lists, asking different students to tell you how to say the numbers. You might like to give further examples of those that caused difficulties.

9   Great Britain quiz

Time: 15–20 minutes
Activity type: Group work
Preparation: Make one copy of page 58 per four students
                  Cut it up into its four sections

Grammar point
Asking questions
Using question words
What is .../Who is .../
Why are ...
Word order of questions
Giving information

Method

1 Tell the class you are going to find out how much they know about Great Britain (and at the same time work on questions).

2 Divide the class into groups of four (any extra students will need to make groups of five). Give each person in the group a different section of the handout (A, B, C or D).

3 Firstly they work alone to rewrite their three questions in the correct word order. When everyone in the group has done this, they can start to ask others in the group their questions. All the answers are given at the bottom of the sheets and have to be matched to the right question.

4 When groups have finished, go through the answers and check that everyone understands. Now give a few minutes for students to study the information. Then ask them to write down all the questions and answers they remember. Congratulate the group who now have the best knowledge of Great Britain.

Key

1 What is the second biggest city in Great Britain? **Birmingham**.

2 How many children does the Queen have? **Four**.

3 Is Ireland part of Great Britain? **No**.

4 What is the head of the government called? **The Prime Minister**.

5 What is the highest mountain in Great Britain called? **Ben Nevis**.

6 How long is the longest river? **354 kilometres**.

7 What is the population of Great Britain? **About 60 million**.

8 How big is England? **130,360 square kilometres**.

9 Where is Cardiff? **In Wales**.

10 What is the capital of Scotland? **Edinburgh.**

11 Why are Oxford and Cambridge famous? **For their universities.**

12 What is in Loch Ness in Scotland? **A monster.**

10 Can you remember?

Time: 20 minutes
Activity type: Asking and answering questions in
                    pairs
Preparation: Make one copy of pages 59 and
                    60 per student

Grammar points
Present continuous
He's running/She's eating.
There is .../There are ...
There are two birds.
Question words
Who/What/How many/Why etc.
Asking questions
*Is the man reading a newspaper or a book?/Who is
waiting at the bus stop?*

Method

1   You might like to start by revising question
words and how to ask questions. Write
some examples on the board. (You could
ask students to ask as many questions as
they can about the classroom e.g. *How
many tables are there? Who is sitting next to
the door?* etc.)

2   Now say you are going to see how good
they are at remembering things and also at
asking questions. Divide the class into
pairs and give each student a copy of the
<u>same</u> picture. (You can start with either
one). One member of the pair is given two
minutes to study and memorize the picture
(no writing) while the other person studies
the same picture and thinks of ten
questions to ask about it (these questions
should be as challenging as possible and
may be noted down). Circulate to help the
question writers as needed.

3   After two minutes, say 'stop' and now the
student who has been doing the
memorizing, turns over their picture and
answers questions asked by their partner.
The questioner should ask ten questions
and note down their partner's score of
correct answers.

4   When this has been done, ask what the
scores were and invite each pair to suggest
some questions.

5   Now give out the second picture and the
roles are reversed with the previous
questioner memorizing and vice versa.
Once more, give two minutes and proceed
as above.

6   You could finish the activity by asking
everyone not to look at either picture and
asking ten questions yourself. They note
down the answers. The class memory
champions merit a round of applause.

11 Two letters

Time: 20 minutes
Activity type: Individual reading and correcting,
                    followed by pair discussion
Preparation: Make one copy of page 61 per
                    pair of students and cut in half

Grammar points
Apostrophes in contractions
I'm afraid I've been busy.
Apostrophes in genitive/possessive forms
My uncle's house
Spelling
Letter writing
Formal style and informal style

Method

1   Divide the class into pairs and give each
member of the pair one of the letters. Look
briefly at the format of each letter,
pointing out where the address and date
go, the beginnings and endings, etc.
Distinguish between a formal letter and an
informal one.

2   Explain that each letter contains mistakes
and it is their job to identify and correct
those mistakes. The informal letter has no
apostrophes and these need to be inserted.
The formal letter has a number of spelling
mistakes which need to be put right.

3   Allow five minutes for students to work
individually on their letters, making
corrections. At the end of this time, say

'stop' and ask them to exchange letters with their partner.

4   Now allow a further five minutes for their partner to check through what they have done and to make any further corrections that may be necessary.

5   When this second check has been completed, ask each pair how many mistakes they found in each letter and write these numbers up on the board. Then tell them the real number of mistakes: eighteen in the informal letter and twenty-one in the formal letter (including some repetitions). Allow more time for pairs to recheck their work if the numbers do not conform.

6   When students (and you) are satisfied they can find no more mistakes, go through the answers (the correct versions appear below).

CORRECT VERSIONS OF LETTERS:

39 Honeywell Road
London N8 9YP

16 June 2000

Dear Maria

Many thanks for your last letter – it's always good to hear from you. Thanks also for the photos of your family – your sister's really pretty and I can see why she's hoping to be a model.

I'm afraid I can't write a long letter today as the school exams are starting tomorrow and I've got to get down to some serious work for my Maths exam. I don't like Maths much, but I must do well if I'm going to study engineering later.

It's my brother's birthday next Saturday and he wants a dog! However as we live in a flat it's not possible and he'll have to be content with a fish. I've bought him a large goldfish and it's hiding under my bed – in its bowl of course! I hope he likes it.

And how are you? I hope everything's going well with your studies and your music. Did you pass your violin exam? Write when you've got time and let's try and meet this summer – perhaps in my uncle's house by the sea.

With lots of love from

Bella

13 March 2000

The Secretary	27 Valley Street
Exeter College of Art	Liverpool
Exeter	ME4 7YT
EX6 8UH	

Dear Sir/Madam

I should be grateful if you could send me some information about the Exeter College of Art as I should like to come to study here in September.

I have studied Art and Design at school and will soon be taking my exams. I hope to do well and become an art teacher in the future. Painting particularly interests me and I enjoy designing posters for the cinema.

Could you also tell me about where I could live in Exeter? Does the college have rooms for students and what is an average rent? I should be glad if you could send me some addresses.

Thank you for your help. I look forward to hearing from you soon.

Yours faithfully

Martin Evans

12 Me and my snake

Time:	25–30 minutes
Activity type:	Discussion in small groups followed by writing a story
Preparation:	Make one copy of pages 62 and 63 per small group of students (3–5) Cut it up into individual pictures and mix these up well (be sure to keep each set together)

Grammar point
Present simple
She goes into a shop. The snake eats the cake.
Discourse – simple story-telling and structuring *then/so/later/in the end*, etc.

Method

1   Introduce the activity by drawing a snake on the board and asking for reactions. Explain they are going to tell the story of a short film about a snake.

2   Divide the class into small groups (3–5 students) and give each group a set of the

cards. Tell them that their job is to arrange these pictures into a logical order to make a short film. Allow them about five minutes to do this.

3   When they have an order they like, give ten minutes for each group to write down the story shown by their picture sequence. This should be written in the present tense and use some simple discourse markers. You might like to suggest some on the board: *The story starts .../Then … so......./Later that day .../In the end … .* Walk round while they are working to help and inspire where necessary.

4   Once groups are ready, ask each one to come out to the front of the class and tell their story (they could also act it out). Compare different versions and choose a class favourite.

5   This activity lends itself well to homework of writing a story entitled 'The Snake' perhaps.

Elementary/Pre-intermediate

13 What makes a good friend?

Time: 20–25 minutes
Activity type: Individual, group and whole class ranking exercise
Preparation: Make one photocopy of page 64 per student

Grammar points
Use of comparatives
This is more important than that./This is less essential than that.
Use of superlatives
This is the most important./This is the least essential.
Expressing opinions
I think/I believe/In my opinion, etc.
Agreeing and disagreeing
I agree/I disagree
Ranking
first/next/before/after

Method

1   Give each student a copy of the handout and explain that they are going to discuss the qualities that make a good friend and rank them in order of the most important. Explain that rank means to give something a position on a scale.

2   To get the ball rolling, you might like to write the following up on the board and invite comment:

A friend in need is a friend indeed. *(English proverb)*

I do not believe that friends are necessarily the people you like best, they are merely the people who got there first. *(Peter Ustinov, 1977)*

3   Go through the fifteen criteria on the handout, reading them aloud and explaining if necessary. Then allow students a few minutes to work individually to rank these in order of importance – 1 is the most important and 15 the least important. They should write these numbers in the first column.

4   When this has been done, students make small groups (4–6) to discuss their rankings. Write the following constructions on the board:

X is more/less important than Y.
X is the most/least essential.
I think/In my opinion/I agree/I disagree
First … Then … Before … After … Last

Encourage them to use these in their discussions.

5   Now allow ten minutes for the groups to discuss and make a new ranking (which they write in the second column) reflecting the general feeling of the group. Circulate to give encouragement and help.

6   When you have stopped the activity, ask if students changed their rankings after group discussion and did they change their opinions much. Proceed to a class ranking, asking each group to participate and

choosing the most common criteria. What else would they add to the list?

7　This lends itself to writing an essay for homework: 'How to be a good friend'.

14　Odd one out

Time:	20–25 minutes
Activity type:	Pair work discussing grammar points
Preparation:	Make one copy of page 65 per pair of students

Grammar points
Verbs
Irregular past tense
Modals
Verbs with the same form as the noun
drink/answer/dance/chat
Uncountable nouns
information/geography/milk/love
Adverbs
quickly/slowly
Irregular plurals
women/children/men/people
Irregular comparatives
better/worse/further/elder

Method

1　Divide the class into pairs and give each pair a copy of the handout. Explain that they have to find the odd one out (i.e., the word that is different to the rest) each time from a grammatical point of view. Do the first one together as an example: the answer is *go* as all the other words are part of the verb *to be*.

2　Give ten minutes for them to do this, circulating to give clues to those who may not be on the right track. Students should write down the odd word out in the second column and briefly explain why in the third column.

3　Collect in all the handouts once time is up (make sure students have put their names on) and redistribute for other pairs to correct. Go through inviting answers and reasons. Scoring is 1 point for finding the correct word and 1 point for giving the

right reason. Finally scores are totalled and the sheets passed back. Congratulate the class champions.

Key

1 *go* – not the verb *to be* **2** *looked* – not an irregular past tense **3** *eight* – not an ordinal number (as used in dates and ordering) **4** *like* – not a modal verb **5** *her* – not plural **6** *win* – not the same form in the past and infinitive **7** *language* – not uncountable **8** *friendly* – not an adverb **9** *adults* – not an irregular plural **10** *eat* – not the same form for the verb and the noun **11** *slower* – not an irregular comparative **12** *happy* – does not use *more* and *most* to make the comparative and the superlative

15　Hungry cities

Time:	25 minutes
Activity type:	Individual work followed by work in threes on a cloze test
Preparation:	Make one copy of page 66 per three students and cut into three

Grammar points
Word order
Present passive
Bread is made./Energy is needed., etc.
Prepositions
of/by/in/to, etc.
Definite article
Adverbs and adjectives

Method

1　Write the title 'Hungry Cities' on the board and elicit what it means. Revise the words: *food/country/town/city/energy/bread/slice/flour*.

2　Divide the class into threes (A, B, C) and give each student a different part of the handout. If there are extra students give them any part.

3　Explain that they all have the same text about feeding cities but there are fifteen words missing in each text and these are not the same fifteen words. First give about five minutes for students to work alone to try to fill in the missing words. Circulate to give help and advice.

4 Now put students into threes making sure each person has a different copy of the text (A, B and C). Any extra students can be integrated into a three.

5 Students take it in turns to read out their text to the other two students, who listen carefully and mark how many words they got right. Then all students work together (only speaking and not looking at one another's texts) to complete the passage correctly.

6 For a whole class round-up, ask individual students to read out sentences and make sure everyone has a correct copy of the full passage. Ask about scores and congratulate those with high ones.

16 A camping weekend

Time: 25 minutes
Activity type: Individual, pair and group discussion with decision-making
Preparation: Make one copy of page 67 per student

Grammar points
Giving reasons
because: We should take a jacket because it might rain.
as: We need a sleeping bag as it's cold at night.
Expressing necessity
need: We need a torch.
Expressing lack of necessity
don't need: We don't need a book.
Infinitive of purpose
We need a candle to see at night.

Method

1 You might like to introduce the topic by drawing a tent on the board and asking if anyone has been camping. Then give everyone a copy of the handout and look at the items in the picture (you may want to check pronunciation). Explain that they are going away for a camping weekend (Friday evening to Sunday evening). Tents are provided but they need to bring everything else they need with them in a backpack.

2 Firstly, students work alone to make a list of the thirty items they would choose from those shown.

3 Once they have done this, they compare their list with a partner and they work together to reduce the number to twenty-five essential items. Before they start, revise how to give reasons and write some examples on the board: *We need a sleeping bag because it's cold at night. We don't need a candle as we have a torch. We should take a large bowl to do the washing up.* Students should use these structures in their discussions.

4 After about five minutes, put two or three pairs together to make a small group whose role is to come up with a final list of only the twenty absolutely vital items.

5 For feedback, you could ask groups to list their twenty items on the board or read them out. They should give reasons for including things and reasons for not including them. You could try to come up with a class list and then ask everyone to say what one extra item they personally could not do without and why.

17 Clues for crosswords

Time: 25–30 minutes
Activity type: Pair work writing clues and then doing a crossword
Preparation: Make enough copies of pages 68, 69 and 70 for half the class (i.e. for a class of 20, make 10 copies of each handout) Cut page 70 (answers) into two

Grammar points
Adverbs
Adverbs of manner: *beautifully/clearly*, etc.
Adverbs of frequency: *always/usually*, etc.
Adverbs of degree: *very/really*, etc.
Adverbs of place: *here/there*, etc.
Adverbs of time: *yesterday/then*, etc.
Position of different types of adverb
She spoke clearly.
He often went home early.
I saw him yesterday., etc.

11

Method

1 Start by revising adverbs – ask for some examples and write these on the board. Then write the following headings on the board: *manner/frequency/degree/time/place*. Ask students to write some examples for each category. Discuss usual position of adverbs in the sentence.

2 Divide the class into pairs and give half the pairs the handout for Student A (empty crossword grid and space for clues) and the other half the handout for Student B. Also give each student their appropriate answer crossword, fully completed.

3 Explain that their task is now to write clues (so that another pair will be able to fill in the empty crossword correctly). They can use pictures or sentences with gaps e.g. *She ran so ... that she won the race. (quickly)*

4 Give about ten minutes for pairs to write clues, circulating to give ideas where needed. Then redistribute crosswords A to pairs B and vice versa.

5 In this second stage, they work to complete the crossword. When finished, they could check with the answer sheet or you could check it as a class. Congratulate those who finished completely – both the crossword-doers and the clue-setters!

Note: This activity can also be done individually i.e., each student has a sheet (half are A and half are B) and writes their clues independently, exchanging crosswords with one other person to complete. This is a quieter and less communicative activity, but may suit certain classes.

18 Be different!

Time:	20–25 minutes
Activity type:	Small group activity; second part whole class teacher-led
Preparation:	Make a copy of page 71 per small group (3–4 students)

Grammar points
Modals
may/might/could, etc.
Use of articles
Comparatives
Conjunctions
if/as/because/since, etc.
Present perfect
Past simple
Adverbs

Method

1 Give each small group a copy of the handout. Explain that they have to work together to find a word (only one each time) to complete the sentences correctly. However, this is not all. They should also aim to find a word that they think nobody else will use (there are different possibilities for each space). They should write their word in the box below.

2 Allow about ten minutes for this and then stop the activity. Now go through each sentence and ask groups for their words. If their word is correct, they get one point and if they are the only group to say that particular word, they get an extra point. Groups write their scores in the boxes and then add them up at the end. The winners will be both grammatically accurate and imaginative!

19 Earth alert

Time:	20 minutes
Activity type:	Group work, communicating by words and pictures
Preparation:	Make enough copies of pages 72 and 73 for each student to have one section (A, B, C or D) Cut each page into two

Grammar point
Numbers and amounts used in comparisons
as much as/as big as/twice as many/35 times
Present simple
go/uses/disappears

Method

1 Introduce the topic by writing 'Earth Alert' on the board and asking students to give you some words connected with this. Try to elicit: *rainforest, pollution, energy, average* and some comparatives: *as much as, six times as much as.* You might like to write the following sentence up for brief discussion: *Breathing air in a polluted city can be as bad as smoking ten cigarettes a day.*

2 Divide the class into fours. Any extra students should work in a pair with a student in a four. Give each person (A, B, C, D) a copy of the appropriate section of the handouts and tell them they must keep what is written on it a closely guarded secret from others in their group.

3 Each person has in front of them a sentence with a fact about an environmental problem and the aim of the activity is to communicate facts to others by writing and drawing.

4 Firstly, each student reads what is in front of them and then illustrates it in the box below (no 1). They should write figures in their picture but cannot use any words or letters.

5 Give a few minutes for this and then instruct students to fold over the sentence so that it cannot be seen. They then pass their picture to the next person in the group. This person studies it carefully and then writes a sentence that they feel expresses in words what they see (in box 2).

6 Once this is ready, they fold over the picture and pass on their words to the next student who illustrates them in box 3.

7 The words are folded over again and the picture passed to the final student in each group who writes their sentence interpreting the picture.

8 Finally the paper is passed back to the student who had the original sentence.

9 At this point, have a whole class round-up. Write each of the four original sentences on the board and ask different groups what

final sentence they ended up with. Congratulate any who came close to the original; others should be good for a laugh.

10 Finally allow a few minutes for papers to be looked at in the group and questions such as: *What is that?/I didn't understand this./This looked like ...,* etc.

20 Spot the differences

Time: 15–20 minutes
Activity type: Pair work
Preparation: Make one copy of page 74 per pair of students and cut in half

Grammar points
Present continuous
Two men are eating burgers.
There is .../There are ...
There are three children at a table.
Asking questions
Is there a woman with a baby?/Are there three men at the door?
Short answers
Yes, there is./No, there aren't.

Method

1 Divide the class into pairs (A and B) and give each member of the pair the appropriate picture. They should not show each other their picture and should sit back to back if possible.

2 Explain that they have pictures that are very similar but not exactly the same. By describing their picture and asking each other questions they will work together to find the differences. Write a few examples of questions and answers on the board as a model, e.g., *Are there three men at a big table? – Yes there are./No there aren't. There are two men at a small table.; Is a woman leaving? – No, in my picture a man is leaving.*

3 Allow exactly eight minutes and then stop the activity (circulate while it is in progress to give help where needed). Ask pairs how many differences they have found and tell them there are twelve. Allow another two minutes for them to try to find everything.

4 Stop and allow pairs to look at each other's pictures and locate all the differences. Ask students to answer individually and write the complete list of differences up on the board. Congratulate those who found them all.

Key

In the second picture: **1** there is a picture of an ice-cream above the counter; **2** there is only one person working behind the counter; **3** the clock says 6.30; **4** the woman next to the clock is not holding a baby; **5** the poster says 'treble-mega-big-burger'; **6** the young girl by the counter is wearing a stripey T-shirt; **7** the woman at the front left-hand table is eating a burger, not fries; **8** there are only two men by the door; **9** the waiter who is cleaning up is not wearing a cap; **10** there are three drinks on the front right-hand table.

21 Perfect partners

Time:	25–30 minutes
Activity type:	Class mingle followed by pair work
Preparation:	Make one copy of page 75 per student

Grammar points
Gerunds
listening to music/washing up, etc.
Use of gerund after certain verbs
like/dislike/don't like: *I like swimming.*
can't stand/hate/detest: *I can't stand not having any spare time.*
enjoy/appreciate/look forward to: *I'm looking forward to having a party.*
Asking questions about likes and dislikes using gerunds
What do you like doing when you're alone?
both
We both enjoy reading.
all
We all hate feeling cold.

Method

1 Write 'perfect partners' on the board and explain that students are going to do an activity to find out who they have most in common with in the class – their perfect partner!

2 Give everyone a copy of the handout and go through the sentences, giving time for people to complete these individually, being as truthful as they can. Before they start, revise the use of the gerund which is used in all these examples. Draw attention to the fact that nearly all verbs of liking and disliking are followed by the gerund. While they are writing, circulate to give help as needed.

3 Now give 10–15 minutes for a class mingle where students get to their feet and question as many of their classmates as they can about their likes and dislikes. Before they begin, revise questions by writing one or two examples up on the board, e.g., *When you're alone, what do you like doing? As far as housework is concerned, what do you detest doing?*

4 Stress that they do not have to note down the answers they receive, but simply to keep a note of how many likes and dislikes they had in common with each person (e.g., Samir 6; Sabrina 3)

5 When most people seem to have got several names to choose from, stop the activity and ask students to make a pair/small group with the person/people they had most in common with.

6 Now they work together to complete the last part of the handout, expressing all the things they had in common.

7 For feedback, invite different pairs/groups to tell the class some of the things they had in common. Is there anything the whole class likes or dislikes?

22 What is it?

Time:	Five minutes per game – several games can be played
Activity type:	Pair work
Preparation:	Make one copy of page 76 for every four students and cut up into twenty sections

Grammar points

Present simple passive used for descriptions
made + of
This is made of cotton.
used + for + gerund
This is used for eating.
used + by
This is used by children.
found + in/at/beside/near etc.
This is found in the bedroom.
Adverbs of frequency
This is usually made of wood./This is sometimes used by doctors.

Method

1 Introduce this activity by hiding a simple everyday object behind your back (e.g. a pen/book/bus ticket, etc.) and giving class clues as to what it is. Use *It's made of … . It's used for … . It's used by … . It's usually found in … .* Write the constructions up on the board (explaining this is the present simple passive if you wish).

2 Now tell them that they are going to play a game where they give clues and their partner must guess what the object is. However, the game has been made more interesting (and challenging) because there are certain words they must not say. Give an example: *gloves (without saying the words gloves/hands/cold) e.g., These are usually made of wool or cotton and are used by everyone in the winter. They are often found in pockets.*

3 Now divide the class into groups of four (preferably) or three. They will play as a pair against the other pair. Give each group a set of the cards face down which they must place on the table in front of them but not look at. .

4 Decide which pair will start and they sit opposite each other (Pair A students 1 and 2). The other pair watch and listen and make sure that the words on the card are NOT said (Pair B).

5 Explain that when you say 'start' Student A1 will pick up the first card from the pile, look at it and show it to Pair B (but NOT to A2, their own partner). A1 will then give

clues as to what the object is, using the structures practised. When A2 guesses the word, A1 puts the card down and A2 picks up the next card (and once again shows it to Pair B) and gives clues as to what it is. Pair A continue like this for two minutes when you shout 'stop'. They then count up how many items they have guessed and the turn passes to Pair B. If a student says one of the words on the card by mistake, they lose that card and also lose one of those they have already guessed.

6 Pair B now have two minutes themselves to do the same and when time is up, the scores are counted and the winners announced.

7 You can play several games with different pairs and also ask students to make up some cards of their own for others to play with (they could write and draw these on the backs of the original cards).

23 Ask Grandma Grammar!

Time:	25 minutes
Activity type:	Mingle and group work
Preparation:	Make enough copies of pages 77 and 78 so that each student has one of the problems to answer; cut out the individual letters.

Grammar points

Use of definite and indefinite articles
the sea/a river
Future idea expressed by present continuous
I'm visiting my mother on Sunday.
There is/There are
There is a woman with a baby.
few/little with countable and uncountable nouns
a little butter/a few apples
Personal pronouns
he/she/it
can/cannot/can't
He can't come this weekend.
Subject and object personal pronouns
Maya and I have the same birthday./She invited Maya and me.
Use of apostrophe (it's/its)
It's a nice day./The cat cleaned its ears.

Method

1 Write the words 'Grandma Grammar's Problem Page' on the board and invite students to tell you what they would expect it to be about. Tell them Grandma Grammar has taken a holiday and so they are going to have to answer the letters she has received this week.

2 Give each student one of the letters (numbers do not have to be equal). They have ten minutes to circulate in the class to tell different people their problem and note down any answers. They should underline the answers they think are true.

3 After this, students should form small groups with others who had the same problem and talk together to come up with the best and clearest answer. They should write this in a few sentences and give some examples.

4 Now proceed to whole class feedback. Each group reads out their problem and their answer. The rest of the class can be invited to comment. Do they find the answer clear and useful? If not, how could it be better?

24 Life stories

Time: 20 minutes
Activity type: Group work
Preparation: Make enough copies of pages 79 and 80 for each group (6 or 7 groups)
                 Make another copy of pages 79 and 80 and cut into individual photos

Grammar points
Past tenses
Past simple
He lived/She worked
Past continuous
While he was studying to be a doctor, his father died.
born
He/She was born …
Sequencing of events

Then she …/Later on, he …/Finally, he …
Dates
In 1997, she …

Method

1 Start by writing a brief biography on the board – this can be of someone you all know and they should try to guess whose at the end. Use the simple past with dates, the past continuous and some adverbs to sequence the events e.g. *He was born in 1955 in the USA. While he was still studying at school, he wrote his first computer program. When he was fifteen, he started his own company. Then in 1980 he developed MS-DOS. Now he is the richest man in the world. (Answer: Bill Gates)*

2 Divide the class into six or seven groups (depending on size of class). Give each group a full intact copy of the two handouts (with all eight photos). Also give each group one of the individual photos (you have previously cut up). Only give out six or seven of the photos. They must not show the individual photo to the other groups but keep it a closely guarded secret.

3 Groups now work together to imagine a life story for the person portrayed in their individual photo and write this down, trying to add as much detail about dates and places as possible. Remind them to use past tenses, dates and some adverbs for sequencing. Circulate to give help and encouragement.

4 When groups are ready, they take it in turns to read out their description and the rest of the class look at the two sheets and say who they think it is. (As at least one photo will not be used, there should be some suspense up to the end!)

5 This activity lends itself well to written homework. Students stick one of the photos in their book and write a life story to go with it.

Pre-intermediate/ Intermediate

25 The London Eye

Time: 20–25 minutes
Activity type: Pair work – personal discussion
Preparation: Make one copy of page 81 per student. Make one copy of page 82 per pair of students and cut in half.

Grammar points
Adjectives followed by prepositions
nice to/talk about/take part in/depend on/shocked by/good at/bad at/impressed by/bored by/anxious about, etc.
Asking for information
What does this mean?/What does this refer to?/Could you tell me about this please? etc.
Explaining
That means/refers to, etc.

Method

1   You might like to start by holding up the picture of the London Eye and explaining that it is a big wheel sponsored by British Airways and erected next to the River Thames in London to celebrate the Millennium. It's called the 'Eye' because it's round and gives you a great view of the capital. Then go on to say: *Would you be afraid of going on this?/I'd be afraid/not afraid of going for a ride. Are you impressed by it?* In the answers focus attention on the use of adjective plus preposition (*afraid + of/impressed + by*)

2   Now divide the class into pairs (A and B) and give each person a copy of page 81 (the London Eye) and the appropriate half of page 82 with ten questions. Explain that they are going to answer these questions about themselves and write the answers in the capsules of the London Eye. Allow time for this and circulate to give help where needed. At this stage, everyone is working individually and they should not discuss their choices with others.

3   When people are ready, explain that they are now going to work in pairs and ask each other to explain what is written in each capsule. You might like to revise appropriate questions: *What does this mean?/What does this refer to?* etc. Remind students that in their answers they will be using adjective plus preposition constructions, e.g. *This is somebody I'd love to talk to./This is something I'm saving up for.* etc.

4   Give about ten minutes for students to discuss their answers together. Then go on to whole class feedback, going round 'the Eye' and asking for interesting or unusual answers to the questions.

26 Let's add some adverbs

Time: 25 minutes
Activity type: Individual and pair work
Preparation: Make one copy of page 83 per student

Grammar points
Position of adverbs
Frequency adverbs before verb
I usually stay …
Adverbs of degree before adjective
completely free
Position in compound tenses
She has just started …

Method

1   Give each student a copy of the handout. Read through the twenty adverbs at the top of the page and then explain that all of them need to be put into the passages below. There are various possibilities but all twenty must be used (and appropriately!). Warn them to be careful of word order!

2   Give about ten minutes for students to work alone to try to fit all the adverbs into the passages. As they finish, pair them up so that they can compare and discuss what they have done.

3 Each pair now works together on a definitive version of where they feel the adverbs are best placed.

4 For whole class feedback, invite some pairs to read out their versions, write them on the board and ask others to comment.

5 You can extend the activity by asking students to find five more adverbs they could fit into the passages. Highlight any particularly interesting examples.

Key

(This is one possible version – there are various other solutions.)

I *usually* stay in during the week as I *always* have such a lot of homework to do. In fact I'm so busy that I *seldom* watch television and I *only occasionally* go on the internet to do research. However, this means I have the weekends *completely* free for going out and having fun! You'll *rarely* find me at home on a Saturday night!

Amy has *just* started learning French so she doesn't speak it very well *yet*. She's going to Paris next year, so she'll *certainly* improve *then*. Her mother speaks it *fluently* but she has *never* been to France. *Perhaps* she'll visit Amy in Paris.

Imogen and Sebastian appear to be *happily* married. They both work *hard* and enjoy it as well as *also greatly* enjoying skiing and swimming in their spare time. They only *ever* quarrel about who does the washing up, so they'll *probably* get a dishwasher for their anniversary!

27 Things that upset me

Time: 25 minutes
Activity type: Ranking activity: first individually, then discuss in pairs and groups
Preparation: Make one copy of page 84 per student

Grammar points
Gerunds
losing, failing, quarrelling
Gerunds used as subjects of sentence

Being late upsets me. People forgetting my birthday upsets me.
Negative use
Not being able to sleep upsets me.
Gerunds used after preposition
I'm upset by people asking to borrow money.
Ranking/comparatives
X upsets me more than Y.
Agreeing and disagreeing
I agree./Yes, so am I etc./I disagree./I don't think so., etc.

Method

1 You might like to introduce the topic by pretending to be upset by something e.g. *I'm upset because I had to wait twenty minutes for a bus this morning. Waiting for public transport really upsets me.* Ask for one or two suggestions from class about what upsets them and write these examples on the board. Draw attention to the use of the gerund and use an example with *not* and *people* e.g., *People not listening to me really upsets me.*

2 Give each person a copy of page 84 and tell them to choose the twelve things in the list that most upset them. They should number these 1–12 with 1 being the most upsetting. Give time for this, circulating to help with understanding if necessary.

3 Once this has been done, put students in pairs to compare their ranking. Write up a few examples of what they should say e.g., *Quarrelling with my family and friends is what most upsets me.*, and revise a variety of ways of agreeing and disagreeing e.g., *Yes, I agree, it upsets me too./I don't agree. Seeing tragic news on TV upsets me more.*, etc.

4 Working in pairs, students now choose the ten things they both find most upsetting and put these in order, writing the ranking order in the appropriate column.

5 Now proceed to the last part of the activity where students work in small groups. Put two or three pairs together for this and give them time to choose the eight things that most upset members of the group and rank them in order.

6 Finally, ask each group to read out its ranking and note these on the board. Compare and contrast and see if you can come up with a consensus. Do we all get upset by the same things ? Let's hope not!

28 If ...

Time: 25 minutes
Activity type: Individual writing followed by some pair work discussion
Preparation: Make enough copies of pages 85 and 86 for half the class

Grammar points
Conditionals
Zero conditional
If you want to make a good impression, you should always look your best.
First conditional
If I go out this weekend, I'll go to the cinema.
Second conditional
If I met Bill Gates, I'd ask him for a job.
Third conditional
If my childhood had been different, I would have been happy.

Method

1 Divide the class into pairs (A and B) and give each a copy of the appropriate handout. Explain that they both have ten conditional sentences but that these are not the same and they need to keep their own handout a secret.

2 If you consider it necessary, do a quick revision of the sequence of tenses in conditional sentences. Otherwise, just alert students to the fact that they need to use the appropriate tense.

3 Now give about ten minutes for students to complete their sentences and write their answers in the boxes in the bottom half of their sheet. Stress that they should write in the boxes and not on the lines, which are for their partners to write on later. Circulate to give help where needed.

4 When people have finished, ask them to tear/cut their handouts in half along the dotted line, keeping the top half for

themselves and giving the bottom half to their partners.

5 The aim now is for the students to try to imagine what the original other half of each sentence was and to write that on the lines. Allow another ten minutes for this.

6 Once both members of a pair have finished, they can work together to compare what each has written with the original sentences. Anyone who managed to get close is given a point and those with the most points are to be congratulated.

7 Finally, go through all the sentences with the whole class, discussing possible answers, looking at how close people got to the originals and highlighting any particularly interesting answers.

29 Conjunctions

Time: 20–25 minutes
Activity type: Oral work in small groups
Preparation: Make one photocopy of pages 87 and 88 per group of 4–6 students Cut these up into squares and phrases, being sure to keep each complete set together

Grammar points
Conjunctions
although, because, but, while, as soon as, etc.
Using conjunctions to join clauses
Children should study hard so that they can get good jobs later.
Conjunctions of time followed by present tenses
Take a jacket with you in case it rains later.

Method

1 Divide the class into small groups (4–6 students) and give each group a set of the twenty-four conjunction cards. Go through the conjunctions briefly, checking that everyone understands them. You might like to ask for examples of any students are not so sure about.

2 Groups should sit around a desk or table and turn all the conjunction cards face down in front of them. Now give out the

set of unfinished sentences (fifteen in all, including three blanks) that should also be placed face down.

3   Explain that the object of the game is to use all the conjunctions to finish the sentences on the cards.

4   Students take it in turns to pick a sentence and place this face up on the table so that all the group can see it. Then they pick a conjunction card and try to finish the sentence, using that conjunction. If they can do this and the rest of the group are satisfied with the accuracy of the sentence, they keep the conjunction card and pick another. They then try to use this second conjunction with the same original sentence. If this is also correct, they keep that conjunction card and continue on. Once they cannot finish the sentence correctly, the turn passes to the next student who picks a new sentence to complete.

5   The game continues in this way until all the conjunctions have been used and the person who has collected the most conjunctions wins.

6   The blank pieces of paper can be used by groups to write sentences to use up any remaining conjunctions if they have been through all the twelve sentences and still have conjunctions on the table.

7   Circulate while play is going on to encourage, give ideas and check accuracy.

8   If the class enjoy this activity, it can be played again as different conjunctions will come up with different sentences so it provides excellent recycling of material in different contexts.

30 Geri the goat

Time:	30 minutes
Activity type:	Pair work and then work in small groups, building sentences and a short article
Preparation:	Make one copy of page 89 per student

Grammar points
Word order
Sentence construction
Use of the simple past
They fled/She attacked
Use of the past perfect
She had eaten/They had planned
Parts of speech
articles/nouns/pronouns/adjectives/verbs/adverbs/ conjunctions/prepositions

Method

1   Give each student a copy of the handout and look at the eight parts of speech and the words listed under them. Explain that they are going to use these words to write sentences and eventually an article about *Geri the Goat*. They can use each word any number of times they like, but should not change it in any way.

2   Firstly, students work in pairs to write sentences using the words. Allow about ten minutes for this and encourage them to write as many as they can.

3   Secondly, put two pairs together to make groups of four. They now read all the sentences and choose the best ones to make into a short article, suitable for a newspaper. Give about ten minutes for this.

4   For whole class feedback, ask a spokesperson from each group to read out their article and invite comments. You might like to compare and contrast what students have come up with. For reference, the original story is printed below (you could do this as a dictation and ask if they prefer this version to their own ideas).

5   This activity lends itself to homework of a short article about a heroic animal.

ORIGINAL STORY

Geri the Goat
Two men who broke into a house and stole valuable paintings were chased by a large goat as they escaped through the garden. The goat, whose name is Geri, attacked them so fiercely that they dropped the paintings and fled in

terror. The family had planned to give Geri to a nearby farm, but now say she will stay with them forever as a pet. The paintings were soon recovered from the garden, but unfortunately Geri had eaten one of them!

31 What do you know about animals?

Time: 20 minutes
Activity type: Speculation individually and in small groups
Preparation: Make one copy of page 90 per student

Grammar points
Probability
It's probably true./It may be true.
Certainty
It's certainly true./It's definitely not true.
Likelihood
It's likely to be true./It's unlikely to be true.
Possibility
It's possible./It might be true.

Method

1 Write a fact about animals on the board e.g. *The most poisonous animal in the world is a frog.*, and invite students to express their opinion on the probability of this statement being true. Elicit a range of constructions (see above) and make sure students are clear about the degree of certainty each expresses. (Note: it's true!)

2 Now say you are going to see if they are animal experts and give each student a copy of the handout. Read through it with the class and allow time for students, working completely individually at this point, to note down a number 1–5 each time according to how probable they think it is that the fact is true. (1 is for certainty that it's true and 5 for certainty that it's false with 2, 3 and 4 expressing the degrees of probability that lie in between.)

3 Students now form small groups (3–5 students) and compare their ratings. They should discuss each animal fact, using the

different structures to give their opinions and alter any they feel they have changed their mind about after discussion.

4 For whole class feedback, ask groups for their opinions on each one (and reasons) before giving the right answer (see below).

5 Afterwards you might like to see how many of the facts they can remember and ask them to research a fact each to bring to the next lesson to talk about.

Key

1 True **2** False – 13 seconds **3** True **4** False – it's the contrary **5** False – cats have over 100 vocal sounds and dogs about 10. **6** True **7** True – and so much so that they could be confused at a crime scene! **8** False – cats are the most popular. **9** True **10** True **11** False – they are on the coat of arms because they cannot walk backwards! **12** False – Ben (males) and Tessa (females) **13** True **14** True **15** False – it's the blue whale

32 Every picture tells a story

Time: 25–30 minutes
Activity type: Work in small groups
Preparation: Make enough copies of pages 91 and 92 to be able to give each student one photo.

Grammar points
Talking about appearances – how things look and seem
look
He looks tired.
look as if/as though
She looks as if she's going to cry.
look like
They look like burglars.
seem
They seem tired.
seem to + infinitive
She seems to want to leave./The children seem to be waiting for someone/She seems to be the boss.
seem + negative
They don't seem to be ready.
there seem/seems
There seems to be a misunderstanding.

21

Teacher's notes

Method

1 Divide the class into four groups and give each student in each group a copy of the same picture. Firstly, they work individually to write five or six sentences about what seems to be happening in their picture. Before they start, discuss the ways to use *look* and *seem* to talk about appearances. Write sentences on the board showing the different structures (as above in the Grammar points) and encourage students to use as varied constructions as they can.

2 Once everyone has some sentences written down, they get together in their groups to compare what they have written (if you have a very large class, it may be better to subdivide groups). Talking together, they come up with the most likely or interesting explanation of their picture and write this out (no more than ten sentences).

3 A spokesperson for each group then comes out to the front of the class, shows the picture and tells/reads their description of it. Invite comments and any other possible explanations.

4 This activity lends itself well to homework. Students stick their picture in their book and then write out a description of it.

33 Questions & answers

Time: 25–30 minutes
Activity type: Individual followed by group work
Preparation: Make one copy of page 93 per student

Grammar points
Question words
why/where/who/how/how many/how much/which/what/whose/when
Formation of questions
Prepositions in questions – at beginning with *wh*-word
In which .../From what ..../To which ...?

Method

1 Give each student a copy of the handout and allow them five minutes to complete the twenty questions by putting in the correct question word each time. Point out that some questions may need a preposition as well and write an example on the board e.g., ... city is the Eiffel Tower? (In which .....? Paris)

2 Once students have filled in the questions, they get into groups (4–6 students) and firstly check that they have all written the same questions. In case of doubt or difference, they should ask you. When they all agree on the questions, they work together to try to find the answers and write these below.

3 When groups have answered all they can, check to see if any group has all the answers. If not, give them five minutes to 'trade' answers. Everyone tries to find somebody to trade an answer with them i.e., if I don't know number 3 and somebody I talk to knows number 3 but does not know number 6, we can exchange answers – they tell me number 3 and in exchange I tell them number 6. The object of this trading period is to complete all the answers.

4 After five minutes, shout 'time' and go through the questions and answers with the whole class. Give those with the most answers a round of applause.

5 Students could make up their own questions for homework – and you could use some of the best in a future lesson.

Key

1 What is .....? The Ganges **2** In which .....? Saudi Arabia **3** Where .....? In Moscow **4** Who .....? Plato **5** How many .....? Four **6** Whose .....? Napoleon's **7** In which .....? Titanic **8** How .....? In degrees (centigrade or Fahrenheit) **9** To which .....? Percussion **10** When .....? 1969 **11** Why/For what .....? Because of/For their universities **12** With which .....? Tennis **13** How many .....? Six **14** On which .....? The river Thames **15** Where/In which country .....? In Holland/The Netherlands **16** From what/Which .....? From French **17** For what/Of what .....? Please Turn Over **18** Which .....? Japan

22

19 What .....? electronic **20** How much .....?
About 5 litres in an adult.

34 Setting out the hall

Time:	25–30 minutes
Activity type:	Information gap – describing plans in pairs
Preparation:	Make enough copies of pages 94 and 95 for half the class

Grammar points

Expressions of position
facing/in front of/round the walls etc.
Expressions of size and shape
the large table/in short rows/in small piles etc.
Imperatives to give orders
draw/add/put
Asking for clarification
Where exactly do I put ...?/Is this right like this? etc.
Confirmation
That's fine./Yes, just like that.
Giving reasons
I put the table there because/so that ...

Method

1   Divide the class into pairs (A and B) and give each student the appropriate handout. Explain that they both have a plan of the same hall, but are going to draw in the top plan a design of how they would organize the furniture for a specific function: a lecture for Student A and a party for Student B.

2   Give five minutes for students to work individually to put the furniture into the top plan in the most effective way for their event. They must keep their work a closely guarded secret. (Encourage the use of pencil rather than pen if you can.)

3   Once this has been done, students start to work with their partners. Allow five minutes for Student A to describe his/her plan and for Student B to draw this in the empty plan at the bottom of the handout. Student A is allowed to see what B is drawing and make any remarks they like to get this as accurate as possible, but they must not touch the drawing or show their

own. Before starting, you might like to revise some of the structures in the above Grammar points list (imperatives/ prepositions of place/giving details and confirmation, etc.)

4   Stop the activity after five minutes and get Student B to start speaking and Student A to start drawing. Circulate to give help as needed and then stop again after a further five minutes.

5   Partners now compare their drawings. Go round and comment, praising those that accurately reflect the original.

6   Finally, sketch two plans of the hall on the board and ask the class to help you to fill them in with the most effective organization of the furniture for the two events.

7   This lends itself to homework: 'My design for ....' with a plan.

35 Life experiences

Time:	30 minutes
Activity type:	Mingle asking questions about life experiences
Preparation:	Make one copy of page 96 per student

Grammar points

Present perfect – questions and short answers
Have you ever touched a snake? Yes, I have./No, I haven't.
Present perfect passive
Have you ever been interviewed?
Have something done
Have you had your portrait painted?/I've never had a tooth extracted.
Past simple
I performed in a concert when I was six.
would like
Would you like to touch a snake?/No, I wouldn't like to fly in a helicopter.

Method

1   You might like to introduce the activity by writing 'Life experiences' on the board and asking students to tell you about the most

exciting or frightening thing they have ever done. Then write a question e.g., *Have you ever ridden an elephant?* and invite answers. If nobody says 'yes' write up a second one e.g., *Have you ever ridden a horse?* In the answers, draw attention to the shift from present perfect to past simple i.e.:

Have you ever ridden an elephant?
Yes, I have.
When did you ride one?
Last year when I was on holiday in India.
Also draw attention to the use of *would like to* i.e.:
Have you ever ridden an elephant?
No, I haven't.
Would you like to ride one?
Yes I would./No, I wouldn't.

2 Distribute the handouts and read through questions with students. Allow them fifteen minutes to circulate round the class asking the different questions (they should ask twelve different people a question each if this is possible). If the first answer is *yes*, they should get details. If it is *no*, they should ask if the person would like to have the experience and note the response. While they are doing this, circulate to encourage and check on the correct uses of the verb tenses.

3 After fifteen minutes, stop the activity and ask students to sit down. Ask each person to choose two facts to tell the class – things that surprised or intrigued them. You can finish with a discussion about experiences – do they all teach us something or are there some we can do without?

36 What kind of person are you?

Time:	25–30 minutes
Activity type:	Two personality quizzes. Individual, pair and group work – writing and responding to a quiz
Preparation:	Make one copy of pages 97 and 98 per pair of students

Grammar points
The second conditional
If I saw an accident, I'd call for help.
If I found money in the street, I wouldn't keep it.
Supposing
Supposing you missed the plane, what would you do?

Method

1 Introduce the topic by asking students if they ever do quizzes in magazines to find out what sort of person they are. Now they are not only going to answer quizzes but also write them. Having whet their appetites, give out the handouts. Half the class will have the quiz about honesty and the other half the quiz about resourcefulness. Point out that each has eight questions with a possible situation and space for three possible reactions to that situation. One reaction has already been given – it is up to them to suggest two other possible reactions.

2 Before they start, revise the 'unreal' conditional (second conditional) and make sure everyone understands the tenses to be used i.e., *if* clause in the past and main clause in the conditional with *would*. Point out that *supposing* is used like *if*.

3 Allow ten minutes for students to write two other answers for each question, using the conditional. They can do this individually or in small groups with others who have the same quiz. Circulate while they are working to offer suggestions and advice. Remind them to work out a scoring system: 3 points for the 'best' answer, then 2 and then 1 or 0 for the 'worst' answer.

4 Once this has been done, students get into pairs – a person with the 'honesty' quiz pairs up with somebody with the 'resourcefulness' quiz. They exchange quizzes and choose their answers. They then hand the quiz back to their partner who gives it a score and writes a comment.

5 Whole class feedback can look at people's scores and see who are the most honest and resourceful.

Intermediate/ Upper Intermediate

37 Good advice

Time: 20–25 minutes
Activity type: Class mingle followed by group work
Preparation: Make one copy of page 99 per four students and one over
                Cut up into the four individual problems

Grammar points
Modals
should/ought to/could/need/must
Giving advice using modals
You should talk to her first./You need to see the headteacher. etc.
Giving advice using the second conditional
If I were you, I'd ...
Making suggestions
Why don't you .../How about ....?
Evaluating using superlatives
The best advice .../The worst advice ...

Method

1   You might like to introduce the topic by writing a short problem on the board and asking the class for advice e.g., *I can't get to sleep at night. I'm always in a rush in the mornings.*, etc. Try to elicit a variety of advice forms, using modals and the second conditional, as well as ways of making suggestions.

2   Now give each person in the class one problem from the handout. (Try to make numbers as equal as possible but they do not have to be the same). This is now their problem and their task is to ask people in the class for advice until they have four different pieces of advice which they should note down under the problem. They will also give advice themselves and should try to use a variety of structures.

3   Circulate during the mingle to encourage and help with vocabulary if necessary. This part should take about ten minutes.

4   Stop the activity and ask people to go into groups with others who have the same problem i.e., all problem 1 people go to one part of the classroom, etc. They now compare the advice they got and draw up a list of the most frequent and least frequent and what they consider to be the best and the worst.

5   In the whole class feedback, each group should read out their problem and then talk about and evaluate the advice they received.

6   This could lead onto a further activity by asking everyone to write a problem on a piece of paper and then pass it to their neighbour for advice. It is then passed on to a second person for different advice and finally back to the original person who says which piece of advice they would actually follow and why.

7   Written homework would further consolidate the various structures.

38 Thinking on your feet

Time: 20–25 minutes
Activity type: Fluency work in small groups
Preparation: Make one copy of page 100 per small group of students (5–7)
                Cut up handout into 20 different sections

Grammar points
Superlatives
worst/most/least/most dangerous/funniest, etc.
Use of present perfect with superlatives
the best I've ever seen/the hottest place I've ever been to, etc.
Asking *wh-* questions in a variety of tenses
When were you .../What is ...? etc.
Fluency

Method

1   Divide the class into small groups (5–7 students) and ask them to sit round a table or desk. Give each group a set of the twenty sentences which they place face down on the table without reading them.

2 Explain that they have questions to answer using the superlative e.g., *What's the best book you've ever read. The best book I've ever read is 'War and Peace'.* They must answer each question in a complete sentence and in no more than thirty seconds.

3 The game now proceeds as follows: one person in each group picks up a question and reads it out to the person next to them. This person has thirty seconds to answer it in a complete and correct sentence, being as truthful as possible. If they do this, they keep the question paper. If not, the question goes back on the table. Play then passes to the next person. The game continues until all the questions have been answered and then the person with the most question papers wins.

4 This game practises fluency as well as a correct use of the superlative and students need to be encouraged to think on their feet. In whole class feedback, go through the questions, asking different groups to talk about the most interesting or unusual answers they had.

39 Odd one out

Time:	20 minutes
Activity type:	Individual followed by pair work discussion
Preparation:	Make one copy of page 101 per student

Grammar points
Plural-form nouns (ending in *s*)
politics/trousers/news, etc.
The future and ways of expressing it
will leave/is leaving, etc.
The definite article
Omission and use in geographical names
the Sahara/Hollywood, etc.
Omission and use with 'at'
at home/at work/at the cinema, etc.
Stative verbs, not normally used in the continuous
remember/know, etc.
Verbs followed by the gerund
enjoy/look forward to/be used to, etc.

Verbs followed by the infinitive
manage/afford/pretend, etc.
since and for: *since last week; for a long time/ages,* etc.
Phrasal verbs
get on/get off, etc.
Position of adverbs of degree
really kind/fairly fast/easy enough, etc.

Method

1 Distribute one copy of the handout to each student. Explain that they have to find the odd one out each time from a grammatical point of view. You might like to do an example on the board e.g., *see take know advise go*: Answer <u>advise</u>, as it's the only one with a regular past tense.

2 First allow students five minutes to work individually to do as much as they can.

3 Then put them into pairs so that they can work together to compare and complete their answers. Allow another five minutes for this.

4 Then take in the handouts (make sure students name them first) and redistribute. Have whole class feedback on the answers and get the markers to score the answers: 1 point for identifying the odd one out and 1 point for knowing the reason. Return papers to the original owners and congratulate the grammar champions.

5 You might like to ask pairs to try to make up their own items and see if the rest of the class can solve them.

Key

1 *trousers*: although all end in 's', only trousers takes a plural verb
2 *he left*: all the rest can be used to express the future
3 *cinema*: all the others have *at* without *the*
4 *hope*: all the others are stative verbs and are not normally used in the continuous form
5 *enjoy*: all the others are followed by the infinitive
6 *enough*: this is the only adverb of degree that comes after the adjective or adverb it is qualifying and not before

7   *Hollywood*: it's the only one not to be preceded by *the*
8   *for*: it does not combine with *get* to form a phrasal verb
9   *want to*: all the rest are followed by the gerund
10 *last week*: all the rest are preceded by *for*

40 What have they got in common?

Time: 20 minutes
Activity type: Oral work in small groups
Preparation: Make one copy of page 102 per small group of students (4–6)
                Cut up into 40 squares (being sure to keep these together)

Grammar points
Comparisons
both
They're both difficult to do./Both of them take a lot of time.
neither
Neither of them is much fun.
Similes using *like*
X is like Y because ...
Gerund as the subject of a sentence
Going on a diet is like a headache – they're both very nice when they stop.

Method

1   Introduce the activity by writing two words on the board and asking the class to find as many similarities between them as possible e.g., *What have being famous and a spider got in common? Being famous is like a spider because it can be frightening at first/because they can both move away fast/because neither is very much liked by many people/because it spins a web to trap you,* etc. Elicit answers using *like/both/neither* and point out how the gerund can be used as the subject of the sentence.

2   Divide the class into small groups (4–6 students per group) and give each group a set of the forty items which they should place face down on the table in front of them. They take it in turns to turn over two cards and make a comparison between the two items on them (thirty seconds

maximum thinking time). If the rest of the group consider their comparison valid, they keep the two cards. If not, the two cards are put face down on the table again. In either case, the turn then passes to the next person.

3   The game continues until all forty items have been used and the person who has collected the most cards is the winner.

4   In whole class feedback, ask for any particularly striking examples and for any that were considered impossible.

    Note: This game can be played a second time once students have warmed up as there are an enormous number of possible combinations.

41 True, false or maybe

Time: 20–25 minutes
Activity type: Individual followed by group work
Preparation: Make one copy of page 103 per student

Grammar points
Using modals to express probability
It might be true./It may be true./It could be true.
Adverbs expressing degrees of certainty
definitely/certainly/probably/likely/unlikely
Agreeing and disagreeing
I agree./I disagree./I think so too./I don't think so either.
Giving reasons
Using a variety of tenses

Method

1   Start by writing a statement up on the board e.g., *The American President Bill Clinton has appeared in an advertisement for hair shampoo.* Ask the class if they think it is *certainly true/could be true/probably false/definitely false*. Elicit different ways of expressing probability using modals and adverbs and invite them to give you reasons for their opinions (**Note**: It is false.).

2   Give a copy of the handout to each student and give the class a few minutes to

read through the statements and decide whether they are true, false or maybe. They should write T, F or M in the column, working individually.

3   Once they have done this, make small groups (3–5 students). They compare their ideas, agree and disagree with one another and then finally decide on their group answer. They should now write a sentence expressing their degree of certainty with each answer, e.g., *It's definitely not true that all the Beatles are now dead./It's probably true that there are 20 million words in English./The most poisonous animal in the world might be a frog,* etc. Before they start, write some constructions up on the board as guidelines: *It's probably/certainly/definitely true/false that … . It might/may/could be true that … . It's unlikely that … .*

4   When people have finished, proceed to marking. Ask each group to read out their sentence before you give the answer. They may like to score and see whose general knowledge (and guesswork) was best.

Key

1 False – Disney is his real name. **2** True **3** False – only John Lennon is dead. **4** True **5** True **6** True **7** False – fear of noise is acoustiphobia and noctiphobia is fear of the night. **8** True **9** False – the world's busiest airport is London Heathrow. **10** True **11** False – there are 14. **12** True **13** False – about 3 million to one. **14** True **15** True

42 A day trip

Time: 20–25 minutes
Activity type: Individual written work leading to group discussion
Preparation: Make one copy of page 104 per four students
                  Cut it into the four sections

Grammar points

Future tenses (active and passive)
They'll visit …/Lunch will be served.
Modals (used to give opinions)
They should …/They mustn't miss …/They can't leave without …

Asking others for their opinions
What do you think? Do you agree?

Method

1   Introduce the topic by saying that an English friend of yours is hoping to visit your country and has asked you to teach her five useful words of vocabulary for her trip. Ask the class which five words they would suggest as being the most useful to a visitor and how they would help with pronunciation.

2   Now give each student one of the sections of the handout. It is not necessary for numbers to be the same, but try to get them as even as possible. Read the first sentence all together: *A group of English university students is coming to your town for a day* and then explain that they have all been asked to help with the organization of certain aspects of this visit. Firstly, students work individually to note down five things they would organize. Allow a few minutes for this, circulating to help with vocabulary if necessary. If your class is multilingual, ask them to write about the place they are studying in.

3   Once everyone has some notes, put students into groups with the other people who have the same assignment as they do. They now compare their answers and talk together to come up with their definitive choice. Remind them that this visit is in the future so future tenses should be used. Also point out the use of modals to give opinions e.g., *The students should walk through the old town./They mustn't miss the clock striking twelve in the cathedral./They can't leave without buying some of our famous chocolates.,* etc. Finally, encourage them to ask one another for their opinions e.g., *What do you think? Do you agree? Do you have any other suggestions?* etc. Allow about ten minutes for this discussion.

4   Finish with whole class feedback, asking each group for their five suggestions and

writing these up on the board, asking the rest of the class to comment.

5   This activity could lend itself to a written homework, in the form of a letter to a friend about to visit, or a page from a travel brochure with a guided tour.

43 Transformations

Time: 15 minutes per activity
Activity type: Pair work information gap activity
Preparation: Make one copy of pages 105 and 106 per pair of students
                  Cut each into two

Grammar points
Present perfect passive
What has been done? New windows have been fitted.
Verbs of transformation
repaint/replace/convert/renovate/remove, etc.
to have something done <u>to</u> something
Has anything been done to the walls?

Method

1   You might like to start the activity by writing the word 'transformations' on the board and asking students what they understand by it. Talk about different types of transformation, including the very British interest in constantly working on your home to improve it. (There are lots of TV programmes in the UK showing 'make-overs' of people's property – sometimes even without their knowledge!)

2   Tell the class they are going to work in pairs on the transformation, inside and out, of a house. Divide the class into pairs and distribute the two halves of Handout 1, showing the exterior of a house. Students <u>must</u> keep their pictures secret from each other. Point out that Student A has a picture of the house before transformation and Student B after transformation; both have some useful vocabulary – nouns for Student A and verbs for Student B.

3   Before they start talking, revise the use of the present perfect passive i.e., *What has*

been done to the door? The door has been painted., etc. Students then talk about their pictures and ask each other questions to discover the ten things that have been done to the house to transform it. Once they have found the ten changes, they can look at each other's pictures to check. Pairs now work together to write ten sentences, using all the verbs given and the present perfect passive to describe what has been done.

4   Stop the activity after about 10–15 minutes and ask different pairs to suggest sentences which you can write on the board. (See below for answers.)

5   Repeat the activity using the pictures of the living room (Handout 2). This time Student A has the transformed picture and the verbs and Student B the original room and the nouns. Students can work with different partners for variety, but ensure that everyone has a turn at being Student A and Student B.

6   If preferred, you could also do the second activity differently i.e., students could work individually on the two pictures and write ten sentences that they then compare with a partner. The second activity could also be usefully given as homework. (In both these cases, you will need to make one copy per student.)

Key (variations are possible)

Exterior

New windows have been fitted. The garden shed has been converted into a greenhouse. An extension has been added to the kitchen. The roof has been renovated. The garden has been landscaped. The vegetable patch has been replaced by a lawn. The path has been widened. A garage has been built. The gate has been repaired. The statue has been removed.

Interior

The fireplace has been blocked up. Central heating has been installed. Fitted carpet has been laid. The walls have been repainted. The posters have been taken down. Abstract paintings have been hung. The mirrors have been polished. The bookcase has been removed. The sofa has been recovered. Curtains have been put up.

44 Parents and children

Time:	20–25 minutes
Activity type:	Individual and group work
Preparation:	Make one copy of pages 107 and 108 per pair of students

Grammar points
Verb + object + *to* + infinitive
I want you to work harder./I'd like you to get up earlier.
Verb + object + infinitive without *to*
You make me turn my music off./You don't let me stay out late enough.
Progressive tenses used with frequency adverbs to show annoyance
You're always criticising my appearance./You're forever being rude.

Method

1 Divide the class into two – parents and children – and give each person the appropriate handout: 'Let's listen to the parents' to the 'parents', and 'Let's listen to the children' to the 'children'. Look at some of the small pictures together and briefly talk about them to activate vocabulary. Here are some suggestions. Parents complain that children are untidy; talk on the phone too long; don't study enough; get up late; don't help with the housework; stay out too late; play loud music etc. Children complain that parents make them tidy their rooms; don't let them stay out late; don't let them listen to loud music; want them to study hard; criticise their clothes; make them babysit for younger brothers and sisters etc. Then write the following four verbs on the board: *want like let make* and elicit some sentences using these to check that everyone knows which take *to* when used with an object and the infinitive (see above in Grammar points) and which do not. Also write up a sentence using the present progressive with a frequency adverb e.g., *You're*

always/constantly/forever telling me to turn my radio off and point out how this is used to express annoyance.

2 Now allow ten minutes for everyone to write as many sentences as they can – parents criticising children and saying what they'd like them to do and not do, while children complain about what their parents make them do and don't let them do. In a smallish class, the groups can work as a whole. In a larger class, it may be easier for students to start by working individually or in pairs and then coming together to compare their sentences.

3 Stop the activity after ten minutes and write 'parents' on one side of the board and 'children' on the other. Ask groups in turn to read out a sentence; if it makes sense give 1 point; if it makes sense and is perfectly grammatically correct, give 2 points. Keep the score on the board until all the sentences have been said and then see who has won!

4 You could extend this activity by asking groups to give reasons for their complaints and for what they do and giving extra points for especially persuasive ones.

5 This could lead to written homework consisting of a conversation between a parent and teenage child.

45 A letter of application

Time:	25–30 minutes
Activity type:	Individual and small group work
Preparation:	Make one copy of page 109 per student

Grammar points
Use of apostrophe
for/since
Non-agreement of adjectives with noun
different nationalities
Use of indefinite article
I'm a student./He's a lawyer.
like/as
to work as a secretary/to work like a horse
who/which

so/such
such a lovely meal/so lovely
Gerund after to
look forward to doing
Ordinal numbers
Word order
Letter-writing style

Method

1 Give out a copy of the letter to everyone and explain that this is a letter of application written by a person whose first language is not English. They have been asked to help by correcting the English and style where necessary.

2 Firstly, students work alone to read through the letter, correcting any mistakes they find. Allow time for this and then put students into small groups (4–6) so that they can compare their work. Go through the letter as a class, asking students to tell you what mistakes they have corrected (see corrected letter below). Encourage them to keep looking for any they have not spotted.

3 Now move on to the second part of the activity, where students work in their groups to complete their letter. They collaborate to come up with the best sentences to write in the spaces, remembering that the aim is to write the most persuasive letter and get the job.

4 Groups now read out their whole letter and the class votes on who they would give the job to (and why). If time permits, you might like to ask for volunteers from each group to come up and be interviewed. Follow-up homework could be a letter of application for a job of their choosing.

Key

3th (3rd) June 2000

Dear Mrs Davies

I should like to apply for the position of Mathematics teacher as advertised in last weeks' (week's) ' English Gazette' and am enclosing my curriculum vitae for you to look _ (look at).

As you will see, I have a degree in Mathematics and a teaching diploma. Although I have only been teaching in Britain since (for) one year, I have considerable experience of working with people of differents (different) nationalities. While I was _ (a) student, I ...

My present position is like (as) a supply teacher covering for colleague which (who) is on maternity leave. She will shortly be able to return to work so I need _ (to) find an other (another) post and I would like to travel. What particularly attracts me in (about) living in Poland is that Warsaw is a so (such a) beautiful city and ...

Apart from my teaching qualifications, I hold also (I also hold) a current driving licence and am computer-literate. I ...

I look forward to hear (hearing) from you soon and would be glad to supply you with any further details you might require.

Your faithfully (Yours sincerely)

Miss Julia Maddondai

46 The perfect picnic

Time: 25–30 minutes
Activity type: Group work discussion
Preparation: Make one copy of page 110 per student

Grammar points
should
We should take sandwiches.
need
We don't need tables and chairs.
suggest
I suggest having our picnic by the sea.
I suggest that we (should) have a midnight picnic.
Rules and regulations
Imperatives
Always take your rubbish home./Never damage the countryside.
Giving opinions
Agreeing and disagreeing

Method

1 Start by writing the word 'picnic' on the board and asking everyone to give you one word they associate with it. Then give each person a copy of the handout and ask them to choose three to five other students

they would like to have a picnic with. Groups should sit together.

2   Explain that they are going to talk together and choose their perfect picnic. Look at the handout and draw attention to the different aspects. Each aspect should be discussed and a decision made – they have to agree! You might like to revise the use of *should*, *need* and *suggest* (as in the above Grammar points) before starting.
Note: Do not do the rules at this point.

3   Allow ten minutes for groups to discuss their perfect picnic, circulating to give help and encouragement. Then stop the activity and ask each group in turn what they have decided. (You might like to suggest a few unusual ideas like a midnight picnic or one where only white food is served, etc.!)

4   The whole class decides on which of the possibilities they would prefer for a class picnic (maybe this could really take place at the end of term if everyone spoke English!!)

5   Now turn attention to the golden rules. Discuss how rules are expressed e.g., using the imperative, not forgetting to show how to start with *Don't* or *Never* to express a negative: *Do …/Always do …/Don't …/Never do … .*

6   Students now work individually to write four rules, comparing these with a partner when they have finished. Ask for suggestions and write these up on the board, e.g., *Never damage the countryside./Always take your litter home./Don't smoke or make a fire./Don't disturb others with radios./Take nothing but photographs and leave nothing but footprints.*

47 Let's make it better!

Time: 25–30 minutes
Activity type: Individual and group work
Preparation: Make one copy of page 111 per person

Grammar points
Word order

Position of adjectives
a lonely old man
Position of adverbs
He ran swiftly and silently.
Subordinate clauses
Conjunctions
Past tenses

Method

1   Distribute the handouts and look at the first sentence: *The man walked along the street.* As it stands, this is a very boring sentence which does not convey any atmosphere or suspense or interest. Ask the class to add some adjectives, adverbs and extra clauses to make a far more interesting sentence – one that would make the reader want to read on and one that conveys an atmosphere. They should write on the lines provided and must stick to one sentence only.

2   Give time for this and then ask for some examples. You might like to write up some of the best as inspiration. Here is a possible version: *It was New Year's Day when the lonely old man walked slowly and painfully along the deserted city street to have a cup of tea and a chat in his favourite cafe only to find that it was closed for the holiday that everyone else seemed to be celebrating.*

3   Allocate one of the four sentences to each person. Try to keep numbers as equal as possible and allow time for students to work on their sentence to make it as interesting and evocative as possible. Remind them they must not change the original words nor their order and must only write one sentence.

4   When this has been done, put students into groups of four with one person who has done each sentence. They now have ten minutes to read their sentences to one another and to work together to combine these sentences into a short story. They will need to write some linking sentences and may need to adapt their original sentences to fit the theme.

5   Stop the activity after ten minutes and ask groups to read out their stories. It may be possible to combine several stories into a more effective whole.

6   Follow-up homework could consist of some other sentences for improvement e.g., The children played in the garden./The sun shone in the sky./The car stopped outside the office./The man went to work every day.

48 Shapes and sizes

Time: 10–15 minutes per design
Activity type: Information gap pair work
Preparation: Make one copy of pages 112 and 113 per pair of students and cut in half

Grammar points
Giving and following instructions
Imperatives
Extend the line/Don't join the two points. etc.
Orders (be + infinitive)
You are to draw a line between the triangle and the square.
must
You must lengthen the line.
Comparatives
The line should be longer/shorter., etc.
Sequencing
Once you've done this .../After that ..., etc.

Method

1   Do a quick vocabulary revision if you feel students need it before starting to describe their designs. You could sketch a quick drawing on the board with triangles, squares, circles, horizontal and vertical lines, straight, wavy and dotted lines and ask students to identify them and then instruct you how to copy the design. Elicit a variety of structures to give instructions as detailed above in the Grammar points.

2   Divide the class into pairs (A and B) and give each member the appropriate section of the first handout – the abstract painting. Student A has to describe the painting (which must be kept a closely guarded secret) to Student B who has to draw it in

the frame. During this part of the activity, Student A can look at the picture B is drawing and make any comments s/he likes to improve it (but only words and no gestures!). Stop the activity after about ten minutes or when most people have finished. Allow Student Bs to look at the original and hold up the copies for class scrutiny. You might like to choose the best 'forger'!

3   For the second part of the activity, Student B will talk and Student A listen and draw. Distribute the two parts of the second handout of the decorated plate. This time, students should sit back to back so that B cannot see what A is drawing (though A can ask questions to get things as accurate as possible). Compare results once again.

4   This could also lead on to homework, where students stick one of the designs (or another of their own choosing) in their books and write a description of it.

Upper Intermediate/ Advanced

49 What makes happiness?

Time: 25–30 minutes
Activity type: Ranking activity – individually then in pairs and small groups
Preparation: Make one copy of page 114 per student

Grammar points
Ranking items on a scale
Comparatives used in ranking
X is more/less important than Y.
Superlatives
Z is the most vital factor./Z has the most influence.
Gerund used as subject
Having children makes many people happy./Being in love doesn't always lead to happiness.
Expressing opinions
To my mind/In my opinion, it's pretty obvious ... etc.
Agreeing and disagreeing
Absolutely!/I couldn't agree more./I'm afraid I don't agree. etc.

Method

1 You might like to introduce the topic by writing some quotations about happiness on the board and asking students which they agree with: 'A large income is the best recipe for happiness I ever heard of.' *(Jane Austen)* 'But a lifetime of happiness! No man alive could bear it: it would be hell on earth.' *(George Bernard Shaw)* 'Happiness is what you make of it.' *(Saying)*

2 Give the handout to each student and ask them to work individually to rank the different factors that contribute to happiness i.e. the factor that they consider most important to happiness should be ranked 1 and the numbers written in the appropriate column. Allow some time for this, circulating round the class to give help and encouragement as required.

3 After a few minutes, ask students to work with a partner to discuss their rankings and come up with a joint ranking of the fifteen most important items in their opinion. Before they start, draw their attention to the use of the gerunds as subjects and revise ways of ranking, using comparatives, e.g., *Having children is far more important to happiness than having lots of interests.* Also revise ways of expressing opinions and agreeing and disagreeing.

4 Give pairs about ten minutes to talk together to come up with a new ranking. They should write this in the second column.

5 Finally put two or three pairs together to make a small group. Now they need to talk to one another to compare rankings and come up with a group ranking of the most important ten factors. Once again, allow about ten minutes for this.

6 The activity ends with whole class feedback. Ask each group to report their list and write these up on the board. Look for similarities and differences and ask students to comment on the reasons for their choices. You might like to collate lists to make a class ranking and then ask students to compare this with their original ranking. Obviously there is no right or wrong in such a ranking which is very subjective, but it could be interesting to ask if students have changed their minds at all as a result of their discussions.

7 This activity lends itself to written homework 'What makes happiness?' with ideas from the lesson and students' personal opinions.

50 Keeping adjectives in order

Time:	30 minutes
Activity type:	Pair work, followed by group discussion
Preparation:	Make one copy of page 115 per student

Grammar points
Position of adjectives
a big beautiful Siamese cat/an expensive gold Swiss watch (see end of activity for brief rules)

Method

1 You might like to introduce the activity by showing the class an object e.g. your watch/a book/a bag, etc. and inviting them to give you a variety of adjectives to describe it. Then ask them to combine two or three, e.g. *It's a small digital watch./It's a large new English book.* At this point, do not discuss rules for the position of adjectives as this is a part of the activity that follows. Simply leave one or two correct sentences up on the board to serve as a model.

2 Give each student a copy of the handout and put them into pairs. They work together to put the adjectives into the correct position and order in the sentences and write the sentences out in the space provided. (They should both do this.) You will probably need to allow about ten minutes for this.

3 Now divide the class into small groups (4–6) and split pairs up so that they each go to form a different group. Groups now

compare their answers and work together to write five rules for the position of adjectives. Allow another ten minutes for this.

4   As a class, first go through the fifteen sentences, asking different students to give you the answer. Then ask each group for their five rules and note these on the board. Do they reflect the usage in the sentences? Work with the class to come up with five basic rules, but remind them that reading and a feel for the language are also vital – there is a point when you have to say that it just sounds right!

Key

1 The delegates filed into the huge conference hall. **2** We need some wooden garden chairs for the summer. **3** Amy looked very smart in her long black leather boots. **4** To celebrate their exam results, the whole class went out for a delicious Chinese meal. **5** I'm planning to change my heavy old computer for a laptop. **6** Have you met Juliette's good-looking new French boyfriend? **7** A long sad Russian novel. **8** The scouts had to camp in a cold dark threatening forest for the night. **9** It's a lovely hot sunny summer's day! **10** He's got four naughty younger sisters at home! **11** Miranda and Peter left the city and moved into a large rambling Scottish farmhouse. **12** What I'd really like for my birthday is a pair of expensive black designer trainers. **13** My little brother has beautiful short curly blonde hair. **14** Rishi bought a new light-weight tennis racket from the sports shop. **15** Thank goodness this is the end of this long difficult grammar activity!

Rules

Note: The rules for adjective order are complicated; here are some of the most basic.

1   Just before the noun come adjectives that tell you what it is for i.e. its function, e.g., a reading room/a badminton racket.
2   Before these adjectives, come those which say what something is made of, e.g., a plastic tennis racket/a glass dining table.
3   Before these categories, come adjectives that tell you where something comes from, e.g., French leather gloves/a Welsh serving dish.

4   Before these, come adjectives of colour, e.g., a blue German velvet riding hat/a brown and white Jersey cow.
5   Other adjectives come before all of these, for example, adjectives that tell you about age, shape, size, number, e.g., a big beautiful orange and red sunset/three small white Persian kittens.

51 Dos and don'ts over here

Time: 20–25 minutes
Activity type: Individual leading to discussion in small groups
Preparation: Make one copy of page 116 per four students and cut up into sections

Grammar points
Giving advice, suggestions and recommendations
advise
I advise you to …/I advise …ing
suggest
I suggest …ing/I suggest (that) you (should) … .
recommend
I recommend …ing/I recommend (that) you (should) … .
Modals
should
You should always be punctual for work./You shouldn't talk about money.
must
You mustn't be rude to your boss.
have to
You don't have to wear a tie for a party.
ought to
You ought to avoid personal questions.

Method

1   You might like to introduce the topic by talking about some cultural mistake that you or somebody you know made when they were in another country e.g. taking chrysanthemums to a dinner party in France as a present for the hostess would cause upset as these flowers are associated with death in France and are usually put in graveyards. Invite students to contribute from their own experience if they can. Go on to say that it is just as difficult for foreigners coming to your country and

that it's interesting to look at our own culture and think of those areas that could cause problems to others who are not used to them.

2   Give each student one of the sections of the handout and ask them to write five pieces of advice that they would give somebody coming to their country for the first time on the topic they have been given. They should write five sentences and use a different construction each time. If necessary, revise: *advise/suggest/recommend/should(n't)/must(n't)/ought to/don't have to* and make sure students understand that some give stronger advice than others. Allow about five minutes for this.

3   Now put students into groups with the other students who had the same topic. If the class is big, it would be a good idea to have two groups per topic. Students read out their sentences to one another and compare their ideas. They work together to decide on the five most important dos and don'ts and how strongly to express them.

4   Finally discuss the results with the whole class, inviting groups to read out what they have got and others to comment. Which do they think are the most vital pieces of advice?

5   This activity lends itself well to written homework, for example, in the form of a letter of advice to a penfriend from a different culture who is coming to work in your country for a few months and wants some hints on how to behave.

52 Let's get it right

Time: 20–25 minutes
Activity type: Pair work
Preparation: Make one copy of page 117
                   per student

Grammar points
since
It's ages since I last saw you.
Tags
I'm late, aren't I?

indeed
She was very tired indeed.
Past perfect
I was wet because I had forgotten my umbrella.
wish
I wish I didn't feel so tired.
Passives
She was questioned by ... /A supermarket has opened.
explain
to explain to somebody
as soon as
Phone me as soon as you get there.
Conditionals
Supposing ... would ...
Suggestions using *why not*
Why not go to bed if you're tired?
Present perfect with *just*
This has just happened.
unless
I'll come unless it rains
already
She had already arrived when I got there.
such with uncountables
It was such nice weather that ... .
Future progressive
By this time tomorrow, I'll be sitting on the beach.

Method

1   Distribute the handout and ask students to work individually to read each sentence and decide whether it is right or wrong. They should put *R* or *W* in the second column to indicate this.

2   Students now find a partner and work in their pairs to see if they agree and to decide how to correct the wrong sentences. They should write their correction in the third column.

3   Ask them to choose the five sentences they are most sure of and put an asterisk beside them (*). This will give them double points if they are right but will subtract five points if they are wrong.

4   Take in all handouts (first reminding students to name them) and redistribute them so that everyone is marking somebody else's work.

5   Go through, asking students to read what is in front of them and say if they agree.

Ask others to comment too before you give the right answer. Students should score the handout in front of them with 1 point for Right or Wrong correctly identified and 1 point for making the correction. If there is an asterisk they double the points (i.e. 2 + 2) but if an asterisked item is answered incorrectly they take five points from the score.

6 At the end, ask students to write the grand total and hand back to the owner. Congratulate the champions.

Key

1 W: It's a long time since you phoned me (we do not use the negative) **2** R (note tag) **3** R (note how *indeed* is used to strengthen an adjective with *very*) **4** W: ... because I had missed the bus (past perfect) **5** R (note tense with *wish*) **6** W: Abigail was questioned by ... (passive) **7** W: Please explain to me ... (explain something to somebody) **8** W: ... as soon as you get the news (conjunction of time followed by present and not future) **9** R: *supposing* is a conditional structure **10** W: why not take .... (*why not* + infinitive without *to* used to make a suggestion) **11** R (present perfect with *just* and passive voice) **12** R (*unless* used instead of *if not*) **13** W: When she was eleven, my sister already knew she wanted to be a nurse. (*already* used with the verb in mid-position) **14** R (*such ... that ...*) and as weather is uncountable there is no *a* in front of it **15** R (future progressive used for an action that will be going on at a specific time in the future)

53 Whatever can have happened?

Time: 25–30 minutes
Activity type: Mingle and group work
Preparation: Make one copy of page 118 per four students and cut into sections

Grammar points
Speculation
Modal verbs with perfect infinitives
can: *What can have happened?*
can't: *She can't have understood what you said.*
could: *She could have got lost.*

may: *She may have lost her way.*
might: *They might have had an accident.*
might not: *She might not have heard the phone.*
must: *They must have had bad news.*

Method

1 You might like to introduce this activity by inviting the class to speculate on some happening in the past, either one that is well known (e.g., *Why did the Titanic sink so fast?*) or one that is personal (e.g., *Why was I late this morning?*). Encourage them to use a range of modals with the perfect infinitive e.g., *You must have got up late./You may have gone to bed late last night./You can't have heard your alarm clock.* etc.

2 Give each student one of the four sections and ask them to read their mysterious happening. Firstly they need to think themselves of the most likely explanation and write it down.

3 Now allow about ten minutes for students to mingle as a class, telling one another their scenario (they should try to express it in their own words and not to read it). They should note down all the different explanations they get and try to collect as many as possible. Remind them to use a variety of modals with the perfect infinitive to express their answers.

4 Then put students into groups with others who have the same mystery and they compare the different explanations they have gathered. They decide on the three most likely explanations and write three full sentences expressing these. They need to take care to use a suitable modal to express the degree of certainty they feel.

5 To round-up, ask groups to read out their mysteries and their three explanations. Ask the rest of the class if these are the most plausible and if not, what else is likely to have happened.

54 Working as copy editors

Time:	20–25 minutes
Activity type:	Checking work for accuracy, individually and some group discussion
Preparation:	Make one copy of page 119 per small group (3–5) You will also need a watch or clock to time one minute.

Grammar points
Spelling
Punctuation
Sentence structure
Paragraphing
Capital letters
Apostrophes
Verb tenses and forms

Method

1   You might like to introduce the activity by writing the words 'copy editor' on the board and asking for suggestions as to what this job consists of. Then explain that such a person reads through a writer's work and makes any necessary corrections to achieve a well-written and accurate text.

2   Divide the class into small groups (3–5) and give each group a copy of the handout. Tell them that the text they see is for publication in a magazine and has just come in from an author who does not write very good English. Their job is to go through it and make all necessary corrections – spelling, grammar, punctuation – to end up with a perfectly correct text.

3   Each member of the group will have turns of one minute to start writing the text out correctly. Time this and shout 'stop' at the end of the minute. Then this student will pass it on to the next person in their group who will also have one minute. This will continue until the text is completely written out correctly.

4   Before everyone starts, explain the scoring. Each group starts with 10 points. The first

group to finish and give their text to you wins 10 extra points. The second group 8, the third group 5, the fourth group 3 and the fifth group 1 point.(Any other groups have no points for speed). When the texts are corrected, one point will be deducted for every mistake not seen and not corrected. Thus groups have to balance speed with accuracy.

5   Now start the activity, saying 'stop' at the end of each minute and making sure the text is passed on. When the first group tells you they have finished, take in their text and award them 10 points. Continue until five groups have finished, award their marks, and then stop everyone.

6   Ask students from the different groups to come up to write out different sentences, or you may wish to ask them to say what changes they made while you write it out. Another solution is to use the answer below and either put it onto an overhead projector or photocopy it to give out. For the marking, one mark is deducted for every mistake not seen or for everything not accurately corrected. Finally take these deductions away from the original scores and congratulate the winning group. This activity should help to focus students' attention on how important it is to read their work through and, in fact, act as their own copy editors.

Key

(Some small variations to punctuation are possible – for example a few extra commas. Spelling corrections are underlined.)

Kirsten Danzig does not like to tell people what she does. If she cannot avoid the question, she says she is a teacher which is partly true. She is a university graduate with qualifications in geography and physical training and she is in charge of the physical training of the staff at the Ministry of the Interior where she has worked for seven years.

In fact Kirsten is one of the few professional female bodyguards and holds the rank of captain. She has protected many famous women and celebrities – from queens and first ladies to pop singers and film stars. On duty, she wears a classic suit and looks like any other smart woman in the crowd.

'I never thought of <u>being</u> a bodyguard,' she says. 'It just happened. I was working in a gym and some bodyguards saw me <u>and</u> asked if I'd like to work with them. Now I wouldn't want to do anything else.'

She does not think she is brave.

'All humans are <u>afraid</u> of something,' she says. 'What is important is to learn to control your fear. I think only of <u>protecting</u> the women I have to accompany and facing challenges gives me a lot of <u>pleasure</u>.'

55 Collocation classics

Time: 25–30 minutes
Activity type: Small groups
Preparation: Make one copy of pages 120 and 121 per small group (4–6)
Cut up and keep together (i.e. in two sets of 24 cards each)

Grammar points
Collocation
Noun + adjective
paper thin/dog tired
Adjective + adjective
stark naked/wide awake
Adjective + noun
heavy traffic/loud noise

Method

1 You could introduce the activity by leaving the classroom door wide open and asking class what the matter is when they notice this. Point out that it is *wide* open and not *big/very* open and that this is an example of collocation (words going together).

2 Divide the class into small groups (4–6) and give each group the two sets of cut-up cards. They should sit round a desk or table and place the cards face down – one set on the right and the other set on the left. Explain that the object of the game is to find the pairs that collocate and that they will do this by taking it in turns to turn

over one card from the left hand pile and then one card from the right hand pile. If they collocate, the student keeps them and has another turn. If not, the cards are turned back over in the same positions and the turn passes to the next student. The person who has the most cards when the game is over has won.

3 You will need to circulate during this game to answer questions from the students to check which words do in fact collocate. If you have a large class, you might like to photocopy the answers below and give these to one or two 'assistants' who will also be able to check collocations for you.

4 For feedback, write all the words from Sheet 1 on the board and ask students to tell you the second part.

5 For further practice, make new groups and proceed as before, but this time, when a student has a pair they must make a sentence with the collocation using a tense given by the rest of the group. Only if this is successful, do they get to keep the cards. For example, *stone + deaf + past perfect = My grandfather had been stone deaf for five years when he died./wide + awake + zero conditional = If you want to feel wide awake in the morning, you need to go to bed early the night before.*

Key

heavy traffic loud noise dog tired stone deaf crystal clear fast asleep pitch dark brand new bone dry paper thin wide awake bitter end all-out war broad daylight dire need thin air rock bottom blind devotion tall order rough deal razor sharp stark naked dirt cheap dead straight

56 Newspaper headlines

Time: 20–25 minutes
Activity type: Group work on newspaper language
Preparation: Make one copy of pages 122 and 123 per four students
Cut up each page into two strips

Grammar points
Grammar rules for newspaper headlines
Incomplete sentences
Added spy scandals
Strings of nouns
Computer company policy switch
Articles and verb *to be* omitted
Flood victims desperate
Special use of tenses, e.g., present simple
Britain preserves pound says PM
Infinitive used with future meaning
Prince to marry secret love
Passive tenses without auxiliary verb
Man questioned by police
A wide variety of tenses and structures for writing articles

Method

1   As the subject of the activity is newspaper headlines and the special grammar rules that apply to them, you might like to bring in an English newspaper and ask students to tell you what they understand by some of the headlines. Then write on the board the examples given in the Grammar points above and focus student's attention on the special rules of grammar that apply.

2   Now divide the class into groups of four (or three) and give each student in each group a different headline which they should keep secret from the others. First they read their headline and then express the same idea in a complete sentence, using no more than three of the original words. They write this sentence in the space provided and then fold over the top of the paper so that the headline can no longer be seen.

3   Now the paper is passed to the next person in the group who reads the sentence and writes a short newspaper article based on the information given (and using their imagination!). They then fold over the top of the paper as before and pass the paper on to the next student who now has the article in front of them.

4   Student 3 now reads the article and writes a headline for it, folding up the paper and passing it on to the last student. Student 4

now opens the paper and compares the two headlines.

5   For whole class feedback, ask students to read out their two headlines and comment on the similarities and differences between them. If you have a large class, it would be better to do this in groups i.e., students with the same opening headline meet up and compare their articles and second headlines, choosing two interesting examples to read out to the class.

57 At what age should you?

Time: 25 minutes
Activity type: Pair work discussion
Preparation: Make one copy of pages 124 and
                  125 per pair of students

Grammar points
should
You should be able to get married when you want.
shouldn't
You shouldn't be able to drink when you're under twelve.
ought to
You ought to be able to smoke if your parents agree.
ought not
You ought not to be allowed to fly a plane at seventeen.
allow/permit
We should allow children to refuse to have medical treatment.
allowed/permitted
Children should not be allowed to buy pets.

Method

1   You might like to introduce the topic by referring to something in your country's legislation about the legal age for doing something e.g., *Do you think it's right that 16-year-olds can get married but not make a will?* Encourage a short discussion and elicit ways of expressing rights and responsibilities (see Grammar points).

2   Divide the class into pairs (A and B) and give each student a copy of the appropriate handout, reminding them to keep it a secret from their partner. Now allow about

five minutes or so for students to work individually to fill in their handout, commenting on the legal age for certain rights in current English law and suggesting a legal age for other rights and giving reasons.

3   When students have done this, they start work with their partner. Student B starts by suggesting legal ages for the first ten activities and gives reasons. Student A says what the actual legal age is in England and whether s/he agrees. It then passes to Student A to suggest a legal age for the next ten activities and give reasons, being told the actual age by Student B. While they are working, circulate to encourage discussion and the use of a variety of verbs and structures.

4   After about 10–12 minutes, bring the discussions to a close and ask pairs to choose two of the rights where they feel most strongly that the legal age (either in England or their own country) should be changed and why.

5   Ask pairs for their opinions and reasons and see if there is a class consensus. Generally do they feel children and young people have enough rights?

6   This topic lends itself well to written homework on children's rights, perhaps in the form of a charter or recommendations.

58 What's your alibi?

Time:	20 minutes for each situation (there are two)
Activity type:	Discussion; preparation in pairs and then question and answer in small groups
Preparation:	Make one copy of pages 126 and 127 per pair of students

Grammar points
Past simple
We left work at six.
Past continuous
We were having dinner at nine o'clock./We weren't alone for more than five minutes.

Past perfect
We hadn't noticed the car earlier.
Past perfect continuous
We had been planning a holiday for months.
Questions in a variety of tenses

Method

1   Divide the class into pairs – half the pairs will be Pair A and half the pairs will be Pair B. There must be equal numbers (A and B), so extra students should make a three. Write the word 'alibi' up on the board and check that everyone understands it.

2   Give each person the appropriate handout. Explain that each pair has a crime they are accused of and a crime they have to question another pair about. They should start by concentrating on the top situation (the car crash). Give them five minutes to prepare, working in their pairs. Pair A will think of questions to ask and Pair B will prepare their alibi.

3   After five minutes say 'stop' and put one Pair A with a Pair B. They should sit as near together as they can to avoid overhearing other groups. Now one of Pair B leaves the room while Pair A questions the remaining member of Pair B and notes their answers. Allow a maximum of five minutes for this. Circulate to listen out for verb tenses and note down any examples which cause difficulty.

4   Then the other member of Pair B comes back into the room and in turn is questioned. Pair A are trying to find flaws in the alibi so can be as probing as they like with their questions. Allow five minutes again and then stop the activity.

5   Go round the class asking each Pair A if they think their Pair B is guilty or not. If they believe them to be guilty, they need to say what flaws in their alibi gave the game away. Finish with some feedback on verb tenses, giving the examples you have noted where there were errors and asking students to correct them.

6   There is another situation so that pairs are reversed and everyone gets a chance to play the different roles and ask and answer questions. This can either be done directly after the first pair or be kept for another day.

59   The nine o'clock news

Time:	25 minutes preparation followed by 5 minutes per group for the presentation
Activity type:	Group work leading to oral presentation
Preparation:	Make one copy of page 128 per group (5–7) Bring a tape recorder and blank tape if you would like to record the presentations for students to listen to themselves afterwards.

Grammar points
Choosing items and giving reasons
Ordering items
firstly/to start/then/after that/followed by/finally/to close, etc.
Verb tenses – active and passive voice
Fluency skills
Pronunciation and intonation – oral presentation

Method

1   You might like to introduce the topic by playing a few minutes of radio news in English and asking for comments about the items chosen and how they were presented.

2   Divide the class into groups (about 5–7) and give each group a copy of the handout. Explain that they are radio producers responsible for the nine o'clock news bulletin and have to prepare their next programme. They have a list of all the possible news items but will obviously have to make a choice about what to include and in what order.

3   Give them ten minutes to talk together to choose their items and decide what order to present them in. Remind them to use a variety of adverbs and expressions to express ordering (see above Grammar points).

4   Once they have chosen the content, groups need at least another fifteen minutes to work on their selected items to expand them by adding what details they wish to make them more real and interesting. They also need to decide who will present them and how. Encourage each person to work in detail on two or three items.

5   Now each group in turn presents their news bulletin. Record these if you can. Students always enjoy listening to themselves and it's a good teaching tool to work on any mistakes in tenses as well as commenting on pronunciation and general clarity and expression.

6   This is a fairly long activity and could be done in two lessons i.e., first lesson to choose items and order and allocate certain items to certain people; homework to finish preparing individual items; second lesson to put it all together and check the timing before proceeding to oral presentations. A third lesson could replay the recordings and invite comments, with a detailed error analysis.

60   Jargon

Time:	15–20 minutes per game (two games)
Activity type:	Pair work followed by small groups
Preparation:	Make one copy of pages 129 and 130 per four students and cut into eight.

Grammar points
Writing definitions
Various verb tenses
Sentence structure and word order
Fluency practice
Discussion and speculation
I think it's more likely to be … .
My guess would be … because … .
This word sounds like … so I'd say … .

Method

1 Write the word 'jargon' on the board and ask what it means (slang and specific vocabulary of a trade, profession, occupation or interest). Explain that they are now going to work in pairs on some English jargon (all the expressions are from a dictionary of jargon and most of them have pretty much entered the language now and would be known – or guessed – by most English speakers). It is expected that they will not know any of these expressions, otherwise this activity is not possible!

As an example of what they will be doing, write *culture fair* on the board and then read out the following definitions, asking the class to listen in silence and then write down what they think the correct definition is (you should repeat the definitions twice):

   1 *A rather derogatory term for traditional local handmade art.*

   2 *Making allowance in tests for the variety of cultural backgrounds of those involved.*

   3 *In animation, making cartoon characters move smoothly and without any jerks.*

   (The right answer is 2 and this is a term frequently used by those concerned with testing.)

2 Divide the class into groups of four and each four into two pairs (Pair A and Pair B). Any spare students should make groups of five.

3 Give all Pair As four of the jargon expressions and Pair Bs another four from Sheet 1. They must keep them a secret and will notice that they are given the correct definition and also spaces to write two further definitions of their own. These other definitions will be incorrect but should sound as plausible and official as possible.

4 Give about ten minutes for pairs to work together to come up with two more definitions for each piece of jargon and to write these in the spaces on their papers.

5 Now the game starts. Each pair takes it in turns to read to the other pair their three definitions and the other pair has to choose the one they think is correct. They should do all eight and keep score. As a round-up, ask for scores and congratulate the winners.

6 A further game can be played with the other eight expressions on Sheet 2 – perhaps with different pairs and on another day.

7 In small classes or if preferred, students can work individually on their definitions and then read them out to another student to guess the right one.

43

Part 2:
Material for photocopying

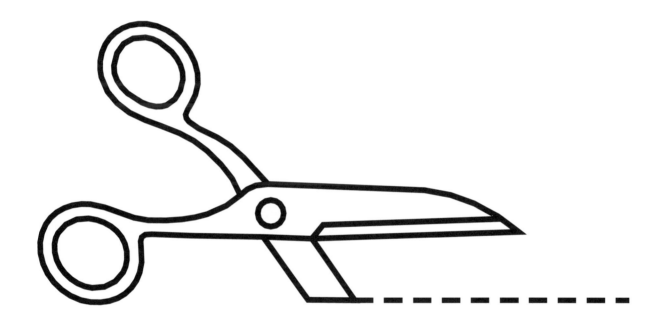

1 Do you agree with me?

Your answers	How many people agree with you?
1 *My favourite sport is*: tennis football running swimming basketball cycling	
2 *My favourite time of year is*: summer spring winter autumn rainy season dry season	
3 *My favourite food is*: pizza rice hamburger fruit fish eggs	
4 *My favourite animal is*: dog cat horse monkey tiger rabbit	
5 *My favourite hobby is*: watching television listening to music going out with my friends reading shopping	
6 *My favourite type of television programme is*: the news sport films documentaries soap operas quizzes	
7 *My favourite colour is*: blue red yellow green black orange	
8 *My favourite type of holiday is*: at the seaside in the mountains staying at home going abroad in a big city	
9 *My favourite number is*: zero one million three the date of my birthday I have no favourite number	
10 *My favourite part of learning English is*: speaking reading interesting passages listening writing stories playing games	

2 Words and stories

During	the	next	week,	the
weather	became	cold.	First	there
was	a	strong	wind	and
then	it	started	to	snow.
Aishling	stood	by	the	window
and	thought	about	her	brother
who	was	coming	home	for
Christmas.	'I	hope	he	won't
be	late,'	she	said	to
her	mother.	'I	don't	want
to	go	to	bed	until
he	comes.'	Just	then	the
phone	rang.			

 From *Grammar Games and Activities 2* by Deirdre Howard-Williams © Penguin Books 2001

3 Questions and answers

First write in the correct word to complete the question.

1 .... is Julia Roberts?

2 .... was Shakespeare's first name?

3 .... Baltic State has Vilnius as its capital?

4 .... many pence are there in £1?

5 .... in the world is Mount Everest?

6 .... is the richest man in the world?

7 .... did man first walk on the Moon?

8 .... mother is the Queen of Great Britain?

9 .... is the British flag called the Union Jack?

10 .... are the colours of the Union Jack?

11 .... is Boxing Day in Britain?

12 .... many planets are there round the Sun?

13 .... did the Titanic sink?

14 .... money is used in Japan?

15 .... does it cost to take a class of ten students together with two
teachers to the cinema if each ticket costs £3.50 for a student
and £4.50 for an adult?

Now try to answer the questions.

1 _____   6 _____   11 _____

2 _____   7 _____   12 _____

3 _____   8 _____   13 _____

4 _____   9 _____   14 _____

5 _____   10 _____   15 _____

Score: _____

From *Grammar Games and Activities 2* by Deirdre Howard-Williams © Penguin Books 2001   **Photocopiable**

4 When's your birthday?

Student A

Month	My estimate	The reality
March		
August		
December		
June		
April		
July		
October		
February		

4 When's your birthday?

Student B

Date	My estimate	The reality
13th		
22nd		
1st		
8th		
30th		
15th		
27th		
3rd		

 From *Grammar Games and Activities 2* by Deirdre Howard-Williams © Penguin Books 2001

 From *Grammar Games and Activities 2* by Deirdre Howard-Williams © Penguin Books 2001

6 Correct the mistakes

Sentence	Right or wrong?	Correction	Score
1 There is two banks in the centre of town.			
2 Mel Gibson is a good actor, isn't he?			
3 I enjoy watching English programmes on television.			
4 This is the most pretty garden I've ever seen.			
5 I would like go to the United States for a holiday.			
6 Sam played tennis so good that he won the match.			
7 How long have you been studying Science?			
8 My sister want to be a doctor.			
9 'What's your father doing? 'He reads the newspaper.'			
10 How much people were watching the big match?			
11 I have a good teacher and I'm understanding Maths better now.			
12 Liz was born in London in 1986.			

7 Crosswords – Write your own clues

Student A

Clues across

1 _____

5 _____

6 _____

8 _____

10 _____

11 _____

13 _____

14 _____

16 _____

17 _____

Clues down

1 _____

2 _____

3 _____

4 _____

5 _____

7 _____

9 _____

11 _____

12 _____

15 _____

 From *Grammar Games and Activities 2* by Deirdre Howard-Williams © Penguin Books 2001

7 Crosswords – Write your own clues

Student B

Clues across

2 _____

3 _____

5 _____

6 _____

8 _____

9 _____

10 _____

12 _____

13 _____

15 _____

Clues down

1 _____

2 _____

3 _____

4 _____

5 _____

7 _____

10 _____

11 _____

12 _____

14 _____

From *Grammar Games and Activities 2* by Deirdre Howard-Williams © Penguin Books 2001   **Photocopiable**   55

7 Crosswords – Write your own clues

Student A: Answers

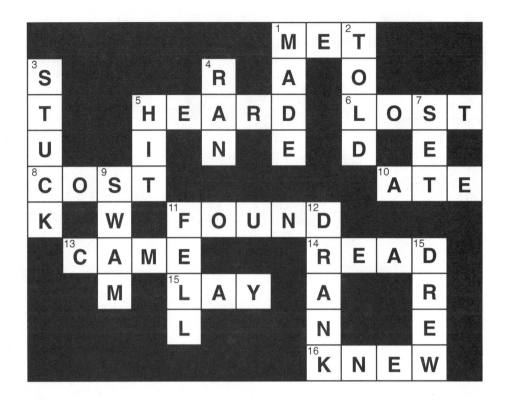

Student B: Answers

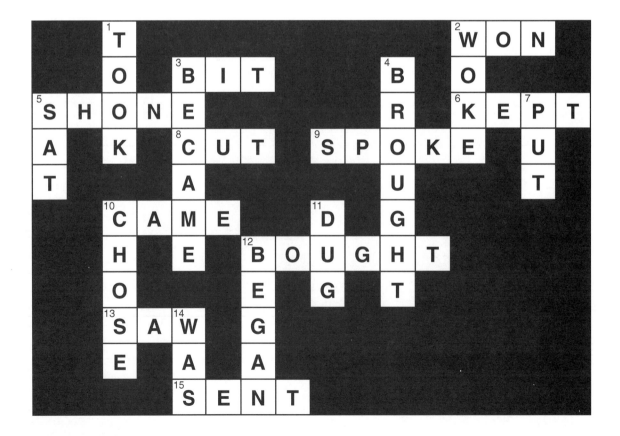

  From *Grammar Games and Activities 2* by Deirdre Howard-Williams © Penguin Books 2001

8 Saying numbers

Student A

Numbers	1,006	11,650	
Dates	2002	1/7/96	
Fractions	$\frac{1}{4}$	$\frac{5}{8}$	
Decimals	2.75	56.04	
Telephone numbers	01876–120013		
Football scores	Manchester United 3 Liverpool 0		
Money	59p $400 5c	£3.13 $5.95	
Kings and Queens	Henry VIII Charles III		
Calculations	$4 + 4 = 8$ $15 - 8 = 7$		
Temperature	$-10°C$		

Student B

Numbers		3,028	10,145
Dates		1966	23/8/2001
Fractions		$\frac{1}{3}$	$\frac{2}{5}$
Decimals		1.25	77.01
Telephone numbers		01557–230213	
Football scores		Arsenal 2 Wolverhampton 0	
Money		80p $100 10c	£4.99 $3.50
Kings and Queens		Elizabeth II Louis XVI	
Calculations		$5 + 15 = 20$ $13 - 8 = 5$	
Temperature		21°C	

9 Great Britain quiz

Questions A

1 in / second / Great / what / biggest / Britain / city / the / is / ?

_____

_____

2 children / many / the / how / does / Queen / have / ?

_____

_____

3 part / Britain / of / Ireland / is / Great / ?

_____

_____

ANSWERS:
Ben Nevis   130,360 square kilometres
A monster

Questions B

4 the / called / head / what / the / is / of / government / ?

_____

_____

5 mountain / the / Great / what / highest / in / called / Britain / is / ?

_____

_____

6 the / long / river / longest / how / is / ?

_____

_____

ANSWERS:
Birmingham   About 60 million
For their universities

Questions C

7 population / is / Great / the / what / Britain / of / ?

_____

_____

8 big / is / England / how / ?

_____

_____

9 Cardiff / is / where / ?

_____

_____

ANSWERS:
Four   The Prime Minister
Edinburgh

Questions D

10 of / what / Scotland / the / is / capital / ?

_____

_____

11 are / Oxford / famous / and / Cambridge / why / ?

_____

_____

12 is / Loch / in / Scotland / what / Ness / in / ?

_____

_____

ANSWERS:
354 kilometres   In Wales
No

 From *Grammar Games and Activities 2* by Deirdre Howard-Williams © Penguin Books 2001

10 Can you remember?

In the street

10 Can you remember?

On the beach

 From *Grammar Games and Activities 2* by Deirdre Howard-Williams © Penguin Books 2001

11 Two letters

Letter A

The apostrophes are missing from this letter.
Can you put them in?

39 Honeywell Road
London N8 9YP

16 June 2000

Dear Maria

Many thanks for your last letter - its always good to hear from you. Thanks also for the photos of your family - your sisters really pretty and I can see why shes hoping to be a model.

Im afraid I cant write a long letter today as the school exams are starting tomorrow and Ive got to get down to some serious work for my Maths exam. I dont like Maths much but I must do well if Im going to study engineering later.

Its my brothers birthday next Saturday and he wants a dog! However as we live in a flat its really not possible and hell have to be content with a fish. Ive bought him a large goldfish and its hiding under my bed - in its bowl of course! I hope he likes it.

And how are you? I hope everythings going well with your studies and your music. Did you pass your violin exam? Write when youve got time and lets try and meet this summer - perhaps in my uncles house by the sea.

With lots of love from

Bella

---

11 Two letters

Letter B

There are spelling mistakes in this letter.
Can you correct them?

27 Valley Streat
Liverpool ME4 7YT

13 Marrch 2000

The Secretery Exeter Colege of Art
Exeter EX6 8UH

Dear Sir/Madam

I shoud be greatful if you could send me some infomation about the Exeter Colege of Art as I shoud like to come to study hear in September.

I have studied Art and Design at sckool and will soon be takeing my exams. I hope to do well and become an art teecher in the future. Painting particularly interrests me and I enjoy designing posters for the cinema.

Could you also tell me about where I could live in Exeter. Does the colege have rooms for studdents and what is an average rent? I shoud be glad if you could send me some adresses.

Thank you for your help. I look forwerd to heering from you soon.

Yours faithfuly

Martin Evans

12 Me and my snake

 From *Grammar Games and Activities 2* by Deirdre Howard-Williams © Penguin Books 2001

12 Me and my snake

13 What makes a good friend?

	Your ranking	Group ranking	Class ranking
1 Someone who always listens to your problems.	_____	_____	_____
2 Someone who will keep a secret.	_____	_____	_____
3 Someone who gives you good advice.	_____	_____	_____
4 Someone who gets on well with your other friends.	_____	_____	_____
5 Someone your family likes and approves of.	_____	_____	_____
6 Someone who shares your interests.	_____	_____	_____
7 Someone who has the same religious or political beliefs.	_____	_____	_____
8 Someone who will always tell you the truth.	_____	_____	_____
9 Someone who has the same background as you.	_____	_____	_____
10 Someone you can meet frequently.	_____	_____	_____
11 Someone who will confide in you about personal matters.	_____	_____	_____
12 Someone who finds the same things funny.	_____	_____	_____
13 Someone of similar intelligence to you.	_____	_____	_____
14 Someone who thinks you are wonderful.	_____	_____	_____
15 Someone you consider to be nice-looking.	_____	_____	_____

From *Grammar Games and Activities 2* by Deirdre Howard-Williams © Penguin Books 2001

14 Odd one out

Words	Odd one out	Why?	Score
1 been is were go are			
2 bought swam looked left went			
3 eight eleventh third nineteenth first			
4 can will like should must			
5 they our we them her			
6 hit put win let split			
7 milk language information love geography			
8 friendly quickly quietly slowly badly			
9 people children adults men women			
10 answer dance chat drink eat			
11 worse slower better further elder			
12 happy interesting exciting beautiful expensive			

15 Hungry cities

Student A

Can you work out .... many breakfasts, ..., dinners and snacks are eaten in your town or .... each day? If every .... eats three meals a day, even a medium-sized town .... 100,000 people will eat almost 110 million meals in a year.

This food is usually grown in the .... and then taken to the towns and cities by trains and lorries. Stores buy .... quantities and then sell the food to customers. A lot of energy is used to make the food we eat.

A loaf of bread is made up of .... 26 slices. Each slice is full of energy. Growing the wheat .... make the bread uses the same energy as you find in 26 slices. Making the wheat into flour uses the .... energy as another 5 slices. The energy .... to bake the .... is equal to 26 slices. One more slice .... energy is needed to transport the .... to the shop. So, it takes the energy of .... slices of bread to make each loaf of 26 slices!

Student B

Can you work out how many ...., lunches, dinners .... snacks are eaten in your .... or city each day? If every person eats three meals .... day, even a medium-........ town of 100,000 people will eat almost 110 million meals in a year.

This food is usually grown .... the country and then taken to the towns and cities .... trains and lorries. Stores buy large quantities and then sell the food .... customers. A lot of energy is used to make the food we eat.

A loaf .... bread is made up of about 26 slices. Each slice is full of energy. Growing the wheat to make the bread uses the .... energy as you find in 26 slices. Making the wheat into flour uses the same energy .... another 5 slices. The energy used to bake the bread is equal .... 26 slices. One .... slice of energy is needed to transport the loaf .... the shop. So, it takes the energy of 40 slices .... bread to make each loaf of 26 slices!

Student C

Can you work out how .... breakfasts, lunches, ... and snacks are eaten in your town .... city each day? If every person eats three meals a ...., even a medium-sized town of 100,000 people will eat .... 110 million meals in a year.

This food is .... grown in the country and then taken to the towns and cities by trains and lorries. Stores buy large quantities and .... sell the food to customers. A lot of energy is .... to make the food we eat.

A loaf of bread is made up .... about 26 slices. Each slice is .... of energy. Growing the wheat to make the bread uses the same energy as you find in 26 slices. Making the wheat into flour uses the same energy as .... 5 slices. The energy used to bake the bread is equal to .... slices. One more slice of energy .... needed to transport the loaf to the shop. So, it takes .... energy of 40 slices of bread to make each loaf of 26 ....!

 From Grammar Games and Activities 2 by Deirdre Howard-Williams © Penguin Books 2001

16 A camping weekend

What would you put in your backpack for a camping weekend?

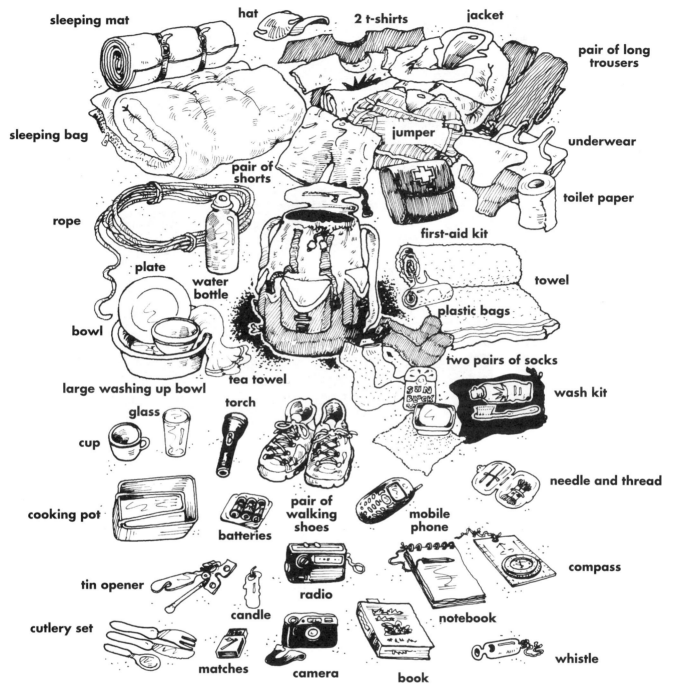

sleeping mat
hat
2 t-shirts
jacket
pair of long trousers
sleeping bag
jumper
underwear
pair of shorts
first-aid kit
toilet paper
rope
water bottle
plate
towel
bowl
plastic bags
large washing up bowl
tea towel
two pairs of socks
wash kit
glass
torch
cup
needle and thread
cooking pot
batteries
pair of walking shoes
mobile phone
tin opener
radio
compass
candle
notebook
cutlery set
matches
camera
book
whistle

Your personal choice of 30 useful items:

Your pair's choice of 25 essential items:

Your group's choice of 20 vital items:

17 Clues for crosswords

Student A

Clues across

2 _____

4 _____

7 _____

8 _____

11 _____

12 _____

13 _____

16 _____

17 _____

19 _____

20 _____

Clues down

1 _____

3 _____

5 _____

6 _____

9 _____

10 _____

14 _____

15 _____

18 _____

   From *Grammar Games and Activities 2* by Deirdre Howard-Williams © Penguin Books 2001

17 Clues for crosswords

Student B

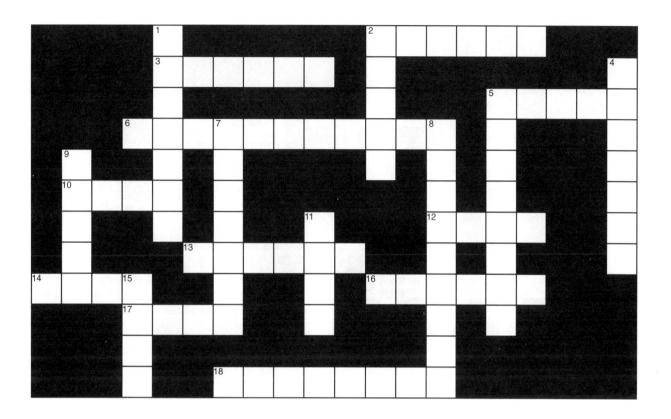

Clues across

2 _____

3 _____

5 _____

6 _____

10 _____

12 _____

13 _____

14 _____

16 _____

17 _____

18 _____

Clues down

1 _____

2 _____

4 _____

5 _____

7 _____

8 _____

9 _____

11 _____

15 _____

17 Clues for crosswords

Student A answers

Student B answers

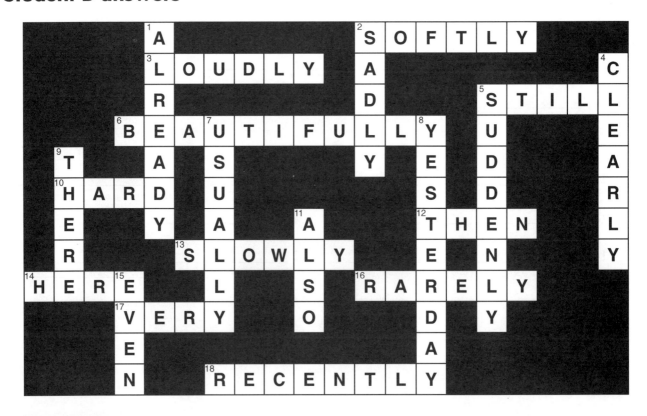

 From *Grammar Games and Activities 2* by Deirdre Howard-Williams © Penguin Books 2001

18 Be different!

Complete each sentence correctly and try to choose a word that you think nobody else will choose. Write only ONE word each time.

1 It _____ rain tomorrow.

2 Vegetarians _____ eat meat.

3 I don't like _____ milk.

4 London is _____ than Tokyo.

5 Have you ever _____ a film star?

6 Someone _____ my car last night.

7 I _____ get up at 7 a.m.

8 The film was _____ exciting.

9 Has Helen _____ her work?

10 Send me an e-mail _____ you have a problem.

11 I'm going home now _____ it's late.

12 We're _____ to catch the 10.15 train to Lisbon.

1	2	3
4	5	6
7	8	9
10	11	12

From *Grammar Games and Activities 2* by Deirdre Howard-Williams © Penguin Books 2001 **Photocopiable**

19 Earth alert

Student A	Student B
One flight from the UK to Sydney in Australia produces as much pollution as a whole year's driving.	The average person in the UK uses 35 times the energy of someone in India.
1 Draw here	1 Draw here
2 Write here	2 Write here
3 Draw here	3 Draw here
4 Write here	4 Write here

 From *Grammar Games and Activities 2* by Deirdre Howard-Williams © Penguin Books 2001

19 Earth alert

Student C	Student D
Twice as many children go to school by car today as ten years ago.	Every year, an area of rainforest as big as England and Wales disappears.
1 Draw here	1 Draw here
2 Write here	2 Write here
3 Draw here	3 Draw here
4 Write here	4 Write here
Student C	Student D

20 Spot the differences

Picture A

Picture B

 From *Grammar Games and Activities 2* by Deirdre Howard-Williams © Penguin Books 2001

21 Perfect partners

All about me

Things I like doing

1 When I'm alone, I like _____

_____

2 When I'm on holiday, I really enjoy _____

_____

3 When I go out to a restaurant, I appreciate _____

_____

4 On my next birthday, I'm really looking forward to _____

_____

5 When I'm tired, I like _____

_____

6 When I go out with my friends, I love _____

Things I don't like doing

7 When the weather's bad, I can't stand _____

_____

8 When I get up in the morning, I really dislike _____

_____

9 When I'm at the cinema or theatre, I hate _____

_____

10 When I have exams, I don't like _____

_____

11 When I get older, I'm not looking forward to _____

_____

12 As far as housework is concerned, I absolutely detest _____

_____

Possible partners and their scores

_____

_____

Perfect partners

We both/all like _____

_____

We both/all really enjoy _____

_____

We both/all dislike _____

_____

We both/all really hate _____

_____

Photocopiable

22 What is it?

Do not say: knife
cut   food

Do not say: fridge
cold   kitchen

Do not say: street
mobile phone   talk

Do not say: pencil
write   paper

Do not say: lamp
light   see

Do not say: bed
sleep   bedroom

Do not say: hat
head   wear

Do not say: socks
feet   warm

Do not say: suitcase
luggage   travel

Do not say: car
drive   road

Do not say: bicycle
wheels   pedal

Do not say: purse
money   keep

Do not say: clean
toothbrush   teeth

Do not say: towel
dry   swimming

Do not say: radio
listen   music

Do not say: computer
keyboard   internet

Do not say: chair   sit
rest

Do not say: bookshelf
books   put

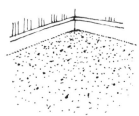

Do not say: carpet
floor   walk

Do not say: watch
wrist   time

     From *Grammar Games and Activities 2* by Deirdre Howard-Williams © Penguin Books 2001

23 Ask Grandma Grammar!

Dear Grandma Grammar,

Please help me! Why do we talk about the sun but a star? Is it a moon or the moon?

Dear Grandma Grammar,

I have a question about the future tense. Is it better to say 'I'm having a party next week. Would you like to come?' or 'I'll have a party next week. Would you like to come?' Or are both correct?

Dear Grandma Grammar,

In an English cookbook, I read 'You need a little milk and a few eggs'. How do you know when to use 'few' and when to use 'little' and can you say 'little eggs'?

Dear Grandma Grammar,

I know 'he' and 'she' are only used for people in English, but what do I use when I talk about my cat, Sooty. Do I say 'she' or must I say 'it'?

23 Ask Grandma Grammar!

Dear Grandma Grammar

When do you use 'there is' and when do you use 'there are'? I'm confused by this sentence: 'There is a man and three children at the door'. Is it correct?

Dear Grandma Grammar

What's the difference between 'can', 'can not' and 'cannot' and what tense are they?

Dear Grandma Grammar

I'm not always sure when to use 'I' and when to use 'me'. Is it 'He gave the tickets to Helen and me' or 'He gave the tickets to Helen and I'?

Dear Grandma Grammar

I know 'it's' has an apostrophe so why is there no apostrophe in this sentence: 'The dog ate its dinner hungrily'?

Photocopiable From *Grammar Games and Activities 2* by Deirdre Howard-Williams © Penguin Books 2001

24 Life stories

24 Life stories

 From *Grammar Games and Activities 2* by Deirdre Howard-Williams © Penguin Books 2001

25 The London Eye

The London Eye is the name of a big wheel on the bank of the River Thames in London. Write your answers to the questions in the capsules.

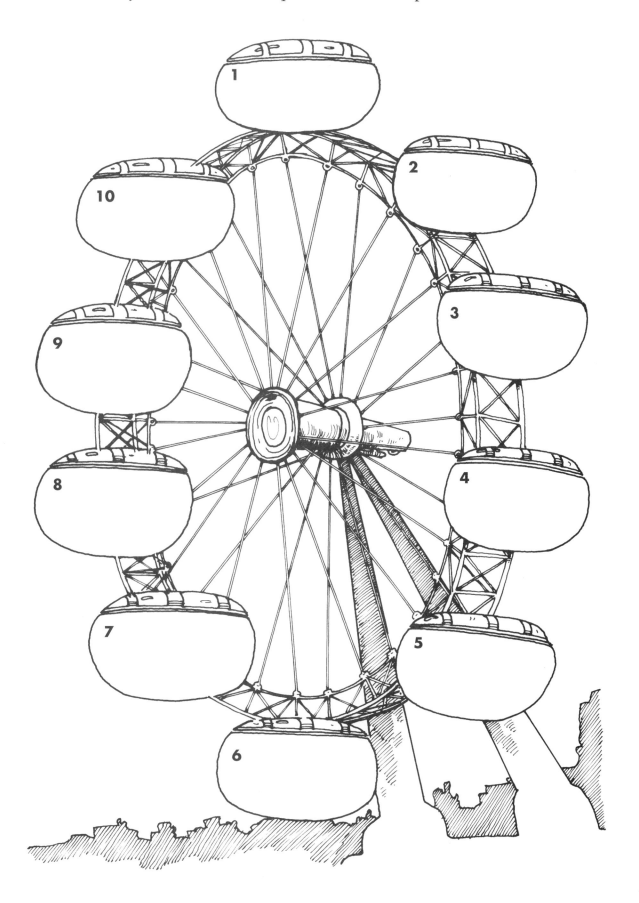

25 The London Eye

Student A

1 Something I'm good at.

2 Something I'm afraid of.

3 A public figure I'm impressed by.

4 A subject or hobby I'm bored by.

5 Something I sometimes get anxious about.

6 Something I have dreams about.

7 Something I would really like to succeed in.

8 A famous person I would love to talk to.

9 Something I am saving up for.

10 A team sport I would not like to take part in.

Student B

1 Something I'm bad at.

2 Something I'm shocked by.

3 A public figure I'm not impressed by.

4 A subject or hobby I'm interested in.

5 Somebody I can always depend on.

6 A subject I like to talk about.

7 Somebody who is usually very nice to me.

8 A team sport I would like to take part in.

9 A word or expression that is typical of me.

10 A person I would like to go on holiday with.

 From *Grammar Games and Activities 2* by Deirdre Howard-Williams © Penguin Books 2001

26 Let's add some adverbs

Where would you place these 20 adverbs in the passages?

just never completely occasionally hard greatly certainly also
usually then happily always perhaps only seldom fluently ever
rarely probably yet

I stay in during the week as I have such a lot of homework to do. In fact I'm so busy that I watch television and I go on the Internet to do research. However, this means I have the weekends free for going out and having fun! You'll find me at home on a Saturday night!

Amy has started learning French so she doesn't speak it very well. She's going to Paris next year, so she'll improve. Her mother speaks it but she has been to France. She'll visit Amy in Paris.

Imogen and Sebastian appear to be married. They both work and enjoy it as well as enjoying skiing and swimming in their spare time. They only quarrel about who does the washing up, so they'll get a dishwasher for their anniversary!

From *Grammar Games and Activities 2* by Deirdre Howard-Williams © Penguin Books 2001 **Photocopiable**

27 Things that upset me

Things that upset me	My ranking	Pair ranking	Group ranking
1 People criticising me.	_____	_____	_____
2 Being late for an appointment.	_____	_____	_____
3 People asking me to lend them money.	_____	_____	_____
4 Seeing tragic news on the television.	_____	_____	_____
5 Waiting for somebody who doesn't turn up.	_____	_____	_____
6 People forgetting my birthday.	_____	_____	_____
7 Not having enough money to buy what I want.	_____	_____	_____
8 Not being able to sleep.	_____	_____	_____
9 Failing a test or exam.	_____	_____	_____
10 Hearing sexist or racist remarks.	_____	_____	_____
11 Quarrelling with my family or friends.	_____	_____	_____
12 Losing something.	_____	_____	_____
13 Not feeling well.	_____	_____	_____
14 Missing my favourite TV programme.	_____	_____	_____
15 Having to wait a long time to be served in a shop or restaurant.	_____	_____	_____

   From *Grammar Games and Activities 2* by Deirdre Howard-Williams © Penguin Books 2001

28 If ...

Student A

Complete these conditional sentences in the **boxes** below.

1 If I could spend a day with someone famous, _____

2 If I had to be another nationality, _____

3 If we had been born fifty years ago, _____

4 If I go out this weekend, _____

5 If our climate here became much hotter, _____

6 _____, people would be much happier.

7 _____, the world today would be very different.

8 _____, we wouldn't be able to use the internet.

9 _____, I'll give you a ring later.

10 _____, I'll scream!

Student A write in the boxes. **LEAVE LINES BLANK FOR STUDENT B**.

1 _____ [   ]

2 _____ [   ]

3 _____ [   ]

4 _____ [   ]

5 _____ [   ]

6 [   ] _____

7 [   ] _____

8 [   ] _____

9 [   ] _____

10 [   ] _____

From *Grammar Games and Activities 2* by Deirdre Howard-Williams © Penguin Books 2001   **Photocopiable**

28 If ...

Student B

Complete these conditional sentences in the **boxes** below.

1 If I ever emigrated, _____

2 If I could change one thing about my life at present, _____

3 If I met Bill Gates, the richest man in the world, _____

4 If I lose my purse and all my money on the way home tonight, _____

5 If most people lived to be over one hundred years old, _____

6 _____, most parents would be very upset.

7 _____, English would be an easier language to learn.

8 _____, our country would attract a lot more tourists.

9 _____, you should always look your best.

10 _____, I would be a very different person!

Student B write in the boxes. **LEAVE LINES BLANK FOR STUDENT A.**

1 _____

2 _____

3 _____

4 _____

5 _____

6

7

8

9

10

From *Grammar Games and Activities 2* by Deirdre Howard-Williams © Penguin Books 2001

29 Conjunctions

WHEN	UNLESS	ONCE	ALTHOUGH
AND	BUT	AS	AS SOON AS
BECAUSE	EVEN IF	AS LONG AS	IN CASE
EVEN THOUGH	IN SPITE OF	UNTIL	PROVIDED THAT
WHENEVER	WHILE	WHATEVER	SO THAT
BEFORE	THAT	SINCE	WHETHER

29 Conjunctions

Maya will be a wonderful doctor ...

Take a jacket with you ...

Samara and Robbie had six children ...

I'll give you a lift to the station ...

I can't come with you ...

It was so hot yesterday ...

I feel like crying ...

Jamie never took holidays ...

Children should study hard at school ...

Don't lend Kate any money ...

Imogen didn't mind working overtime ...

We'll book our next holidays ...

 From *Grammar Games and Activities 2* by Deirdre Howard-Williams © Penguin Books 2001

30 Geri the goat

ARTICLES	NOUNS		PRONOUNS	ADJECTIVES
the a	garden goat name farm Geri one	terror paintings men house family pet	they them she who whose	two valuable large nearby

VERBS		ADVERBS	CONJUNCTIONS	PREPOSITIONS	
say stay had eaten escaped stole dropped were chased to give	attacked planned broke fled recovered is will	unfortunately fiercely soon now forever so	but and as that	from by through in of	into to with from

Now use the words to make as many sentences as you can.

_____

_____

_____

_____

_____

_____

_____

_____

_____

31 What do you know about animals?

Facts about animals

1 Snails can sleep for three years without eating. ☐

2 The longest recorded flight for a chicken is thirteen minutes. ☐

3 A duck's quack does not echo. ☐

4 It's possible to lead a cow downstairs but not upstairs. ☐

5 Dogs have more vocal sounds than cats. ☐

6 Tigers have striped skin as well as striped fur. ☐

7 The fingerprints of koala bears are almost indistinguishable from those of humans. ☐

8 The most popular pet in Great Britain is a rabbit. ☐

9 An ostrich's eye is bigger than its brain. ☐

10 The muzzle of a lion is like a fingerprint and no two lions have the same pattern of whiskers. ☐

11 Emus and kangaroos are on the Australian coat of arms because they are both only found in Australia. ☐

12 The most popular dog's name in Great Britain is Prince. ☐

13 A female sheep is called a ewe. ☐

14 A rat bite can be fatal. ☐

15 The largest mammal is an African elephant. ☐

Probability rating

1 = It's certainly true.
2 = It's probably true.
3 = It's possible – it might be true.
4 = It's unlikely to be true.
5 = It's definitely not true.

From *Grammar Games and Activities 2* by Deirdre Howard-Williams © Penguin Books 2001

From *Grammar Games and Activities 2* by Deirdre Howard-Williams © Penguin Books 2001

33 Questions & answers

1 _____ is the sacred river of India?

2 _____ country is Mecca?

3 _____ is the GUM department store?

4 _____ wrote 'The Republic'?

5 _____ strings does a violin have?

6 _____ white horse was called 'Marengo'?

7 _____ film did Leonardo di Caprio freeze to death in the sea?

8 _____ is temperature measured?

9 _____ section of the orchestra does the drum belong?

10 _____ did the first man walk on the moon?

11 _____ are Oxford and Cambridge famous?

12 _____ sport do you associate Wimbledon?

13 _____ players are there in a volleyball team?

14 _____ river is London situated?

15 _____ would you be if you were speaking Dutch?

16 _____ language does the word 'picnic' originally come?

17 _____ is P.T.O. an abbreviation?

18 _____ country's flag is a red circle on a white background?

19 _____ does the 'e' in e-mail stand for ?

20 _____ blood is there in the human body?

Answers

1	6	11	16
2	7	12	17
3	8	13	18
4	9	14	19
5	10	15	20

From *Grammar Games and Activities 2* by Deirdre Howard-Williams © Penguin Books 2001   **Photocopiable**   93

34 Setting out the hall

Student A

You are organizing a lecture by a well-known author and expect to have an audience of about 100. Decide how to arrange the furniture in the best way and draw this in the plan below.

Complete this plan of the hall, according to what your partner tells you.

 From *Grammar Games and Activities 2* by Deirdre Howard-Williams © Penguin Books 2001

34 Setting out the hall

Student B

You are organizing a party to take place at the end of term in the hall and are expecting about 100 guests. Decide how to arrange all the furniture in the best way and draw this in the plan below.

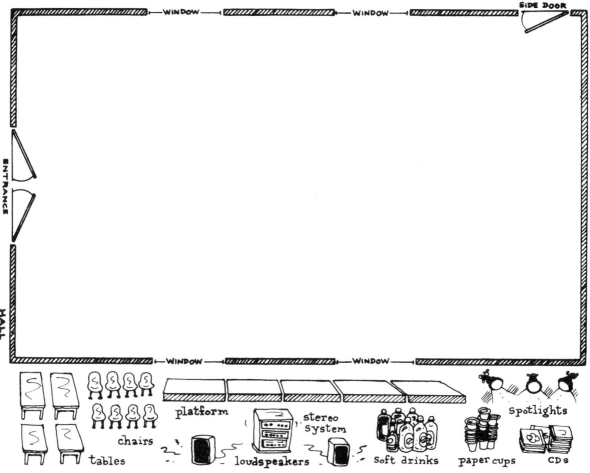

Complete this plan of the hall, according to what your partner tells you.

From *Grammar Games and Activities 2* by Deirdre Howard-Williams © Penguin Books 2001

35 Life experiences

Have you ever ...?	If YES, when?	If NO, would you like to?
1 ... ridden a roller-coaster?		
2 ... had your fortune told?		
3 ... been interviewed?		
4 ... had a tooth extracted?		
5 ... flown in a helicopter?		
6 ... had your portrait painted?		
7 ... caught a fish?		
8 ... touched a snake?		
9 ... performed in a play or concert?		
10 ... witnessed a crime?		
11 ... saved someone's life?		
12 ... read somebody's mind?		

From *Grammar Games and Activities 2* by Deirdre Howard-Williams © Penguin Books 2001

36 What kind of person are you?

How honest are you?

1 If you got the bill in a restaurant where you had just had a rather bad meal and noticed that you had not been charged for your main course, what would you do? (i) I would ask to see the manager and point out the mistake. (ii) (iii) **Score:**	2 If you were staying with friends you did not know very well and accidentally spilt a small amount of ink on the bedroom carpet, what would you do? (i) I'd say nothing and hope they wouldn't notice. (ii) (iii) **Score:**
3 If while waiting for a teacher in her office, you noticed the exam papers for the following day on her desk, what would you do? (i) I'd tell the teacher she should be more careful with security. (ii) (iii) **Score:**	4 If on a business trip your travel expenses were paid in advance by your company, but you got a free lift from a friend, what would you do? (i) I'd do some overtime without pay so that I could keep the money without feeling guilty. (ii) (iii) **Score:**
5 You have been invited to the theatre by somebody you really do not like. However, it is a show you particularly want to see and it's almost impossible to get tickets. What would you do? (i) I would accept the invitation and enjoy the show. (ii) (iii) **Score:**	6 Supposing you got promotion at work because of writing a very good report, but this was largely the work of a colleague who was on sick leave, what would you do? (i) I'd talk to the colleague and ask him if I could do something for him in exchange – that way we'd both benefit. (ii) (iii) **Score:**
7 If you were at a charity fair to raise money for disabled people and noticed an item for sale that you happened to know was an antique and very underpriced, what would you do? (i) I'd buy it myself – after all it's a bargain and somebody else would buy it if I didn't. (ii) (iii) **Score:**	8 At work/school you are allowed to use the computers for educational purposes only. Would you also use them for surfing on the internet for fun? (i) No, I wouldn't because somebody else might be waiting to use the computer. (ii) (iii) **Score:**

Final score and comments:

From *Grammar Games and Activities 2* by Deirdre Howard-Williams © Penguin Books 2001 **Photocopiable**

36 What kind of person are you?

How resourceful are you?

<table>
<tr>
<td>

1 You have invited three people to dinner and made a special meal. However, there has been a misunderstanding and one turns up with her partner. What would you do?

(i) I'd say I was on a diet and eat very little myself.

(ii)

(iii)

Score:

</td>
<td>

2 If you found a small puppy wandering alone in the street near your home with no collar on, what would you do?

(i) I'd leave him alone as dogs can bite and be dangerous.

(ii)

(iii)

Score:

</td>
</tr>
<tr>
<td>

3 If you were at a picnic and wasps were spoiling everyone's pleasure, what would you do?

(i) I'd suggest ignoring them and getting on with the picnic as quickly as possible.

(ii)

(iii)

Score:

</td>
<td>

4 Supposing you spilt coffee on your clothes on the way to a very important interview, what would you do?

(i) I'd buy some new clothes and change into them in the shop.

(ii)

(iii)

Score:

</td>
</tr>
<tr>
<td>

5 If you saw somebody being robbed on a train, what would you do?

(i) I'd ask if I could borrow somebody's mobile phone to ring the police.

(ii)

(iii)

Score:

</td>
<td>

6 If when coming home in a taxi late at night, you suddenly realized you didn't have enough money to pay the fare, what would you do?

(i) I'd say I felt sick and had to get out of the taxi immediately.

(ii)

(iii)

Score:

</td>
</tr>
<tr>
<td>

7 If you were walking in the countryside and your companion suddenly broke his ankle, what would you do?

(i) I'd stay with him until somebody came along.

(ii)

(iii)

Score:

</td>
<td>

8 Supposing you were on your way to a friend's party when you suddenly remembered it was her birthday and you hadn't bought her a present, what would you do?

(i) I'd tell her I hadn't bought anything because I wanted to ask her if there was anything she particularly wanted.

(ii)

(iii)

Score:

</td>
</tr>
</table>

Final score and comments:

 From *Grammar Games and Activities 2* by Deirdre Howard-Williams © Penguin Books 2001

37 Good advice

1 Your problem is your best friend. Recently she's had various problems in her life and is always ringing you up to pour her troubles into your sympathetic ear. However, you've got rather tired of listening to all this late at night especially when you have to get up early next day. Besides, you don't feel you can really help as she doesn't seem to listen to your advice and you're just getting depressed yourself. What can you do?

_____

_____

_____

_____

2 Your problem is a colleague at work. She's always having time off saying she's ill, but you know this is not true as friends of yours have seen her out shopping. These absences cause difficulties at work as it means more work for you and the boss gets annoyed. Should you report her to your boss?

_____

_____

_____

_____

3 Your problem is your daughter. She goes to a school where the other children and their families all have a lot more money than you do. She has started to be upset about this and has refused to have anything second hand. She needs a new tennis racket and says she'd rather not play tennis than have a cheap or second-hand one. You just don't have the money for a good quality one and don't know what to do.

_____

_____

_____

_____

4 Your problem is your boyfriend/girlfriend. You're planning to get married next year but recently he/she has become very irritable and is always finding fault with you. You know he/she has been under a lot of stress as his/her mother is quite seriously ill, but you just don't enjoy being with him/her any more and don't know if you should call the wedding off.

_____

_____

_____

_____

38 Thinking on your feet

Who is the best sportswoman you know?	Who is the youngest person you know personally?
What is the most frightening film you have ever seen?	What is the most dangerous thing you have ever done?
What is the most expensive thing you have ever bought?	What is your least favourite type of food?
What do you like most about your best friend?	What do you find most difficult to remember?
What do you like least about learning English?	Who is the best actor you have ever seen?
What's the most boring conversation you've ever had?	Where's the most interesting place to visit in your country?
What's the funniest thing that has happened to you in the last month?	What's the most embarrassing thing that has happened to you in the last month?
What is the worst thing you've ever eaten?	What's the first word you spoke as a child?
Where's the hottest place you've ever been?	Where's the coldest place you've ever been?
What are you least looking forward to in the future?	What are you most looking forward to in the future?

 From *Grammar Games and Activities 2* by Deirdre Howard-Williams © Penguin Books 2001

39 Odd one out

	Odd word out	Why?	Score
1 news trousers mathematics politics billiards			
2 he leaves he will leave he will be leaving he left he's leaving			
3 church home work school cinema			
4 remember know hope recognize understand			
5 enjoy afford manage pretend offer			
6 really so enough very fairly			
7 Pacific Hollywood Baltic United Kingdom Sahara			
8 for up down on off			
9 look forward to object to want to be accustomed to be used to			
10 three years ages a long time last week a month			

From *Grammar Games and Activities 2* by Deirdre Howard-Williams © Penguin Books 2001 **Photocopiable**

40 What have they got in common?

A cabbage	E-mail	February	Wasps
Love	Getting a good education	Taking an exam	The future
A headache	Politicians	Being an only child	Feeling hungry
Los Angeles	Peace	A classical CD	A fridge
Cows	Modern art	Fashion	Eating ice-cream
A long walk	Getting married	Making money	Going on a diet
A designer-label T-shirt	Hope	Soap	The year 2000
Learning to play the violin	A box of chocolates	Life	A field of corn
Being bilingual	Doing the washing up	Thick snow	Music
Work	Birthdays	Going to the dentist	Crime

 From *Grammar Games and Activities 2* by Deirdre Howard-Williams © Penguin Books 2001

41 True, false or maybe

	True, false or maybe	Sentence
1 Walt Disney's real name was Walter Dirondyke.		
2 Maria Callas, the famous opera singer, was Greek.		
3 All the members of the Beatles pop group are now dead.		
4 Madonna is the singer's real first name.		
5 A person who is interested in UFOs (unidentified flying objects) is called a ufologist.		
6 The collective noun for a group of actors is a company.		
7 Someone who has a fear of noise has noctiphobia.		
8 More people speak Spanish than Arabic.		
9 The busiest airport in the world is John F Kennedy Airport in New York.		
10 There is a hotel in Florida that is completely underwater.		
11 There are more than forty bones in our fingers.		
12 The most recognized clothing brand name in the world is Levi Strauss.		
13 The chances of being attacked by a shark are about one million to one.		
14 The most poisonous animal in the world is a frog.		
15 There are 20 million words in the English language.		

42 A day trip

Sightseeing

A group of English university students is coming to your town for a day. You have been asked to organize their sightseeing and choose five sights for them to visit over about four hours.

1

2

3

4

5

Catering

A group of English university students is coming to your town for a day. You have been asked to organize their food and drink. What five specialities would you choose to serve them?

1

2

3

4

5

Shopping

A group of English university students is coming to your town for a day. You have been asked to take them shopping for souvenirs. What five local items would you choose to show them?

1

2

3

4

5

Culture

A group of English university students is coming to your town for a day. You have been asked to organize a short talk for them about your culture. What five subjects would you choose to present?

1

2

3

4

5

  From *Grammar Games and Activities 2* by Deirdre Howard-Williams © Penguin Books 2001

Student A   Our house before its transformation

(Useful nouns: garden shed, extension, roof, vegetable patch, garden, windows, path, lawn, gate, statue, garage)

Student B   Our house after its transformation

(Useful verbs: fit, add, renovate, convert, landscape, replace, widen, build, remove, repair)

43 Transformations

Student B   Our living room before its transformation

(Useful nouns: sofa, central heating, fireplace, posters, abstract paintings, curtains, mirrors, walls, bookcase, fitted carpet)

Student A   Our living room after its transformation

(Useful verbs: put up, polish, remove, lay, install, block up, repaint, hang, recover, take down)

     From *Grammar Games and Activities 2* by Deirdre Howard-Williams © Penguin Books 2001

44 Parents and children

Let's listen to the parents

44 Parents and children

Let's listen to the children

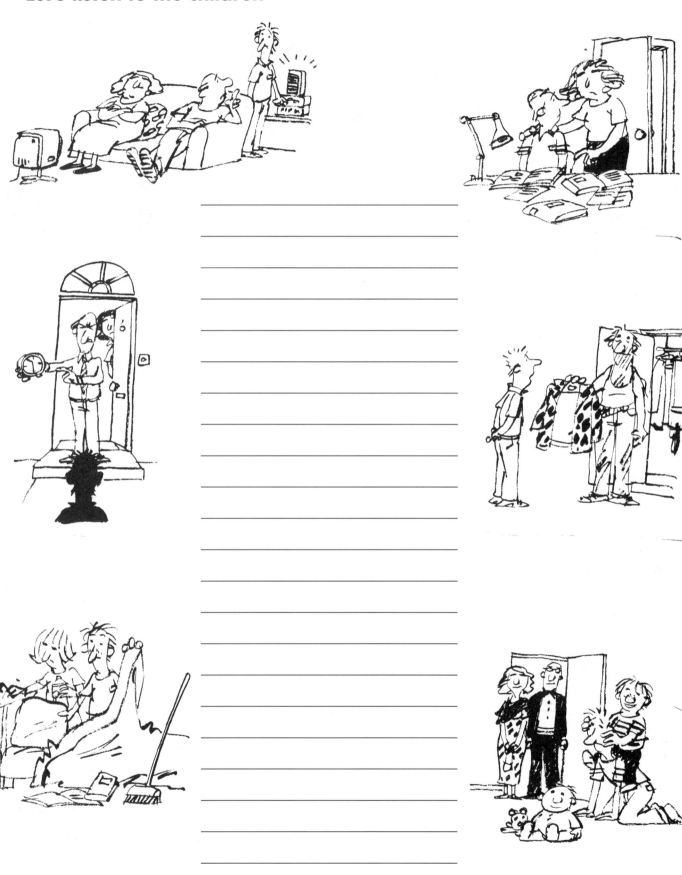

_____

_____

_____

_____

_____

_____

_____

_____

_____

_____

_____

_____

_____

_____

_____

_____

_____

_____

_____

_____

_____

 From _Grammar Games and Activities 2_ by Deirdre Howard-Williams © Penguin Books 2001

45 A letter of application

2 Winspan
Terrace
Edinburgh EY5 2PL

Mrs G. Davies
Director
The International School
Warsaw
Poland

3th June 2000

Dear Mrs Davies

   I should like to apply for the position of Mathematics teacher
as advertised in last weeks' 'English Gazette' and am enclosing
my curriculum vitae for you to look.

   As you will see, I have a degree in Mathematics and a teaching
diploma. Although I have only been teaching in Britain since one
year, I have considerable experience of working with people of
differents nationalities. While I was student, I _____

_____

_____

_____

   My present position is like a supply teacher covering for a
colleague which is on maternity leave. She will shortly be able
to return to work so I need find an other post and I would like to
travel. What particularly attracts me in living in Poland is that
Warsaw is a so beautiful city and _____

_____

_____

_____

   Apart from my teaching qualifications, I hold also a current
driving licence and am computer-literate. I _____

_____

_____

_____

   I look forward to hear from you soon and would be glad to
supply you with any further details you might require.

Your faithfully

Julia Maddondai

Miss Julia Maddondai

46 The perfect picnic

The place: where will you have your picnic?

_____
_____
_____
_____

The equipment: what will you take?

_____
_____
_____
_____

The food and drink: formal or easy to eat?

_____
_____
_____
_____

The arrangements: how to get there and what to do?

_____
_____
_____
_____

Golden rules for safe and considerate picnics

1

3

2

4

From *Grammar Games and Activities 2* by Deirdre Howard-Williams © Penguin Books 2001

47 Let's make it better!

Make these sentences more interesting

Example: **The man walked along the street.**

_____ the _____ man walked

_____ along the _____

street _____ .

---

1 The bus stopped and a girl got off.

---

2 The door was opened by a woman.

---

3 The dog ran into the park.

---

4 There was a boy standing outside the school.

---

48 Shapes and sizes

Student A: An abstract painting

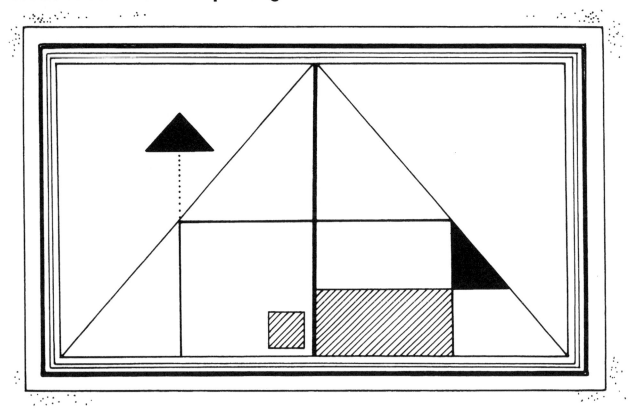

Student B: An abstract painting

   From *Grammar Games and Activities 2* by Deirdre Howard-Williams © Penguin Books 2001

48 Shapes and sizes

Student B: A decorated plate

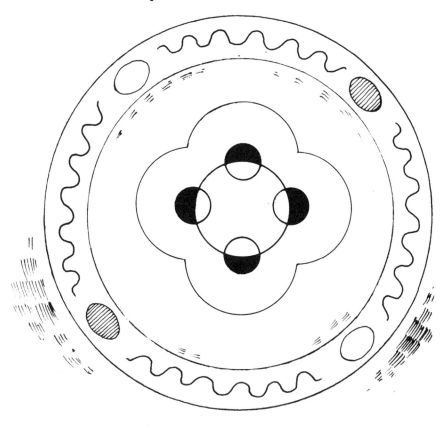

Student A: A decorated plate

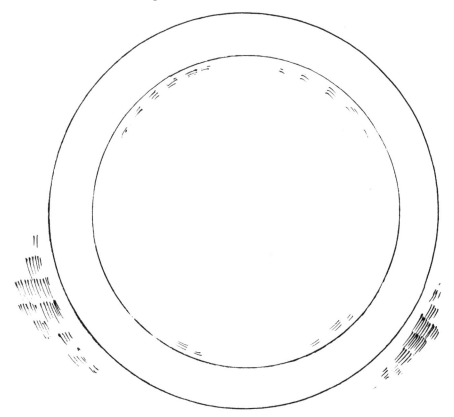

49 What makes happiness?

	Your ranking	Pair ranking	Group ranking
1 Being in love.	_____	_____	_____
2 Having a secure job.	_____	_____	_____
3 Coming from a happy family background.	_____	_____	_____
4 Having good physical health.	_____	_____	_____
5 Living in a country that is at peace.	_____	_____	_____
6 Having enough money to live on.	_____	_____	_____
7 Not having to depend on anyone else financially.	_____	_____	_____
8 Having lots of friends.	_____	_____	_____
9 Having children.	_____	_____	_____
10 Being successful in your professional life.	_____	_____	_____
11 Having a nice home of your own.	_____	_____	_____
12 Being able to see the funny side of even difficult situations.	_____	_____	_____
13 Having lots of interests.	_____	_____	_____
14 Having a positive mental attitude.	_____	_____	_____
15 Having a strong religious faith.	_____	_____	_____
16 Feeling you are making a difference in the world.	_____	_____	_____
17 Feeling good about yourself.	_____	_____	_____
18 Having interesting holidays.	_____	_____	_____
19 Being able to help others.	_____	_____	_____
20 Counting your blessings and realizing there are others much worse off than you.	_____	_____	_____

 From *Grammar Games and Activities 2* by Deirdre Howard-Williams © Penguin Books 2001

50 Keeping adjectives in order

Write the following sentences out again with the adjectives in the correct positions and in the correct order.

1 The delegates filed into the hall. (conference/huge)

2 We need some chairs for the summer. (garden/wooden)

3 Amy looked very smart in her boots. (black/leather/long)

4 To celebrate their exam results, the whole class went out for a meal. (Chinese/delicious)

5 I'm planning to change my computer for a laptop. (old/heavy)

6 Have you met Juliette's boyfriend? (good-looking/French/new)

7 What are you reading? A novel. (sad/Russian/long)

8 The scouts had to camp in a forest for the night. (dark/cold/threatening)

9 Let's go out – it's a summer's day! (sunny/lovely/hot)

10 Poor Ciaran doesn't get much peace – he's got sisters at home! (younger/four/naughty)

11 Miranda and Peter left the city and moved into a farmhouse. (large/Scottish/rambling)

12 What I'd really like for my birthday is a pair of trainers. (expensive/designer/black)

13 My little brother has blonde hair. (curly/short/beautiful)

14 Rishi bought a racket from the sports shop. (tennis/light-weight/new)

15 Thank goodness this is the end of this activity! (difficult/grammar/long)

51 Dos and don'ts over here

Give advice to somebody coming to work in your country for the first time.

Dos and don'ts about what to wear for work and play.	**Dos and don'ts about how to behave at a dinner party.**
(clothes/appearance/jewellery, etc.)	(punctuality/presents/conversation/food, etc.)
1	1
2	2
3	3
4	4
5	5
Dos and don'ts about how to act with the opposite sex.	**Dos and don'ts about how to address people you meet.**
(inviting/paying/politeness/equality, etc.)	(titles/surnames/first names/greetings, etc.)
1	1
2	2
3	3
4	4
5	5

 From *Grammar Games and Activities 2* by Deirdre Howard-Williams © Penguin Books 2001

52 Let's get it right

If there's a mistake, correct it and see your score rise.

	Right or wrong?	Correction (if any)	Score
1 It's a long time since you didn't phone me.	_____	_____	_____
2 I'm still in time for the film, aren't I?	_____	_____	_____
3 Pravina was very pleased indeed to receive an invitation.	_____	_____	_____
4 I explained I was late because I have missed the bus.	_____	_____	_____
5 I wish I didn't have to work so hard for my exams.	_____	_____	_____
6 Abigail was questioning by the immigration officer when she went to New York.	_____	_____	_____
7 Please explain me how to work the new video.	_____	_____	_____
8 Will you let me know as soon as you'll get the news?	_____	_____	_____
9 Supposing you lost your job, what would you do?	_____	_____	_____
10 You look tired – why not to take a break for an hour or two.	_____	_____	_____
11 A new cinema has just been opened in the centre of town.	_____	_____	_____
12 She'll take the job unless the hours are too long.	_____	_____	_____
13 Already when she was eleven, my sister knew she wanted to be a nurse.	_____	_____	_____
14 It was such nice weather that we had lunch in the garden.	_____	_____	_____
15 At nine o'clock this evening, I'll be watching the news.	_____	_____	_____

Grand total: _____

From *Grammar Games and Activities 2* by Deirdre Howard-Williams © Penguin Books 2001   **Photocopiable**   117

53 Whatever can have happened?

Mystery number one

Julia and Richard Griffiths with their three small children hire a canal boat for the day in late summer. When they fail to return by nightfall, a search is organized and the boat is discovered only two miles away, drifting empty, with all their personal possessions still on board. What happened?

Theories:

Mystery number two

You have invited a friend for dinner and she is now over forty minutes late. She phoned you about an hour ago from the station, which is five minutes walk from your house, just to ask you if you needed her to buy anything and you told her no. Where is she?

Theories:

Mystery number three

For your best friend's birthday, you gave her a CD of dance music which you know she likes, but she hardly thanked you at the time and hasn't spoken to you since. Why?

Theories:

Mystery number four

You have just got back to your flat after three days away, to find that all your plants have died and your cat has not eaten its food and has disappeared. What went on in your absence?

Theories:

 From *Grammar Games and Activities 2* by Deirdre Howard-Williams © Penguin Books 2001

54 Working as copy editors

Working as copy editors, make all necessary corrections to this text: spelling, punctuation, paragraphing and capital letters, as well as checking the grammar.

Kirsten: professional bodyguard

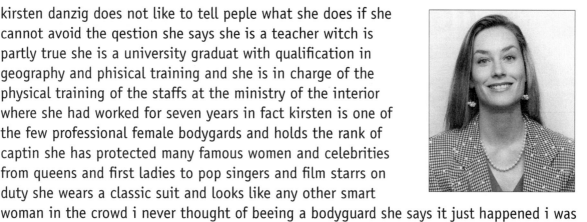

kirsten danzig does not like to tell peple what she does if she cannot avoid the qestion she says she is a teacher witch is partly true she is a university graduat with qualification in geography and phisical training and she is in charge of the physical training of the staffs at the ministry of the interior where she had worked for seven years in fact kirsten is one of the few professional female bodygards and holds the rank of captin she has protected many famous women and celebrities from queens and first ladies to pop singers and film starrs on duty she wears a classic suit and looks like any other smart woman in the crowd i never thought of beeing a bodyguard she says it just happened i was working in a gym and some bodyguards saw me an asked if id like to work with them now I wouldnt want to do anything else she does not think she is brave all humans are afrad of something she says what is important is to learn to control your fear i think only of protect the women i have to accompany and facing challenges gives me a lot of plesure

_____

_____

_____

_____

_____

_____

_____

_____

_____

heavy	loud
dog	stone
crystal	fast
pitch	brand
bone	paper
wide	bitter
all-out	broad
dire	thin
rock	blind
tall	rough
razor	stark
dirt	dead

thin	need
devotion	tired
end	dark
cheap	bottom
clear	noise
traffic	order
awake	daylight
war	straight
deal	asleep
deaf	new
dry	air
sharp	naked

56 Newspaper headlines

RAIL CHIEF QUITS OVER BLAZE DRAMA DEATH	Police probe soap star drug rumours
The sentence:	The sentence:
The article:	The article:
The headline:	The headline:

From *Grammar Games and Activities 2* by Deirdre Howard-Williams © Penguin Books 2001

56 Newspaper headlines

Transport pay cut riots: PM calls for calm	BRITON SOUGHT AFTER FOILED KIDNAP BID
The sentence:	**The sentence:**
The article:	**The article:**
The headline:	**The headline:**

57 At what age should you?

Student A

Rights and responsibilities	Age now in English law	Do you agree?
You can go into a pub but you cannot buy or drink alcohol there.	14	
You can work full-time if you have left school.	16	
You can become an MP or local councillor.	21	
You can live with a relative with your parents' consent.	any age	
You can see a U category film unaccompanied.	5	
You can become a street trader.	17	
If you are adopted, you can see your birth certificate on application to the Registrar General.	18	
You can consent or refuse consent to surgical, medical or dental treatment.	16	
You can get a part-time job with certain restrictions, for example, you cannot work for more than two hours on a school day or on a Sunday.	13	
You can open a bank account if the bank thinks you understand the nature of banking transactions.	at any age	

Rights and responsibilities	Age you recommend	Reasons for recommendation
You can apply for access to personal information held about you on computer files or in a computerized system.		
You can be tattooed.		
You can hold a pilot's licence.		
You can make a will.		
You can buy a pet.		
You can buy fireworks.		
You can drink alcohol in private, for example, at home.		
You can donate your body to science without parental permission.		
You can change your name.		
You can have your fingerprints taken by the police.		

  From *Grammar Games and Activities 2* by Deirdre Howard-Williams © Penguin Books 2001

57 At what age should you?

Student B

Rights and responsibilities	Age you recommend	Reasons for recommendation
You can go into a pub but you cannot buy or drink alcohol there.		
You can work full-time if you have left school.		
You can become an MP or local councillor.		
You can live with a relative with your parents' consent.		
You can see a U category film unaccompanied.		
You can become a street trader.		
If you are adopted, you can see your birth certificate on application to the Registrar General.		
You can consent or refuse consent to surgical, medical or dental treatment.		
You can get a part-time job with certain restrictions, for example, you cannot work for more than two hours on a school day or on a Sunday		
You can open a bank account if the bank thinks you understand the nature of banking transactions.		

Rights and responsibilities	Age now in English law	Do you agree?
You can apply for access to personal information held about you on computer files or in a computerized system.	at any age	
You can be tattooed.	18	
You can hold a pilot's licence.	17	
You can make a will.	18	
You can buy a pet.	12	
You can buy fireworks.	16	
You can drink alcohol in private, for example, at home.	5	
You can donate your body to science without parental permission.	18	
You can change your name.	18	
You can have your fingerprints taken by the police.	10	

58 What's your alibi?

58 What's your alibi?

Pair B
Your alibi for the crime you are accused of

You have been accused of driving dangerously at about 9p.m. last night and smashing into a shop, causing considerable damage to its stock including some antique china. It was your car, but you were not driving. You forgot to lock your car and it disappeared from where you had parked it some time last night. This morning you found it parked in a different place and badly damaged. You spent the whole evening together, having dinner and planning your next summer holidays.

You will have to answer questions individually.

Notes:

Pair B
The crime you have to investigate

A large software company has reported the disappearance of some valuable computer files last night. Only very few people had access to them and you are now going to question two of them. The company say the information could be very valuable to a competitor and must be recovered before the loss becomes public.

You are the detectives charged with finding out who did it.

Notes:

59 The nine o'clock news

You are the producers of a five-minute radio news broadcast that goes out at nine o'clock every evening. Choose from the following news items which you would include and in what order. Then prepare your five-minute programme – you can have several presenters and include interviews if you like.

American child poet gets £100,000 in book deal	Tennis – no Britons in the quarter finals
Polls closed as country heads for democracy	Football fans promise good behaviour in return for tickets
Forest fires hit South of France – family feared dead	Boxing to be banned in all youth clubs after damning medical report
AIDS epidemic – no let-up say World Health	Pop star gives 5 million to saving the rainforest but won't pay council tax
Computer virus hits White House – Pentagon fears for national security	Elephant twins born in London zoo – first for fifty years
Drought forecast for Ethiopia – send help now beg aid agencies	Royal family set up internet site
German schoolgirl takes teacher hostage over exam results	House prices set to rise by more than 10% this month
Top Spanish star in sex scandal	Babies born in the summer less prone to depression in later life claims study
Human gene that causes cancer identified in European breakthrough	GCSE results best ever – standards continue to rise says Education minister
Prime Minister to become a father for the fifth time	More tax relief for families – single parents to benefit
Florida dolphin has own answerphone with recorded 'voice' message	Snow promised for Christmas Day by long-range forecaster
Youth Hostel blaze in Lakes – batteries dead in fire alarms	All lottery numbers under ten this week – no winners

From *Grammar Games and Activities 2* by Deirdre Howard-Williams © Penguin Books 2001

60 Jargon

green room	ride shotgun
1 A room offstage where actors can relax and entertain their friends. 2 3	1 2 To be ready for any eventuality in business. 3
cattle call	daily double
1 2 A mass audition attended by large numbers of hopeful actors. 3	1 A bet that chooses the possible winners of two of that day's horse races. 2 3
vox pop	optical wand
1 2 Interviews conducted at random with men and women in the street to get their views on a certain topic. 3	1 An electronic device that is used in supermarkets to read the barcodes on products. 2 3
bucket shop	peanut gallery
1 2 3 An unlicensed travel agent who buys bulk lots of aircraft seats and sells them cheap to the public.	1 2 3 The highest gallery in a theatre with the cheapest seats.

From *Grammar Games and Activities 2* by Deirdre Howard-Williams © Penguin Books 2001 **Photocopiable** 129

flagship sites	voice wrap
1 Leading stores on which a retailer concentrates his energies and publicity as a showplace. 2 3	1 2 The use of a newscaster's voice to introduce a item which is then narrated by a reporter. 3

magic bullet	lame duck
1 2 3 A drug that can destroy disease and cancers without harming the rest of the body.	1 Someone who holds an office and who cannot be re-elected to that office. 2 3

straw poll	hard news
1 2 3 A quick poll of the nearest voters to get an idea of the results of an election.	1 Important information that appears on the front page of newspapers and leads radio and TV news programmes. 2 3

inherited audience	white land
1 2 An audience who have been watching one TV programme and will simply watch the next without bothering to change channels. 3	1 Land which has been left untouched. 2 3

     From *Grammar Games and Activities 2* by Deirdre Howard-Williams © Penguin Books 2001

Index to structures used

The numbers indicate the activities in which the structures and functions are practised.

PENGUIN ENGLISH PHOTOCOPIABLES

0 582 42785 1

0 582 42784 3

0 582 46563 X

0 582 46564 8

0 582 46158 8

0 14 081562 7

0 582 42783 5

0 582 45146 9

0 582 45145 0

0 582 46901 5

0 14 081632 1

0 14 081656 9

0 582 44774 7

0 14 081619 4

0 582 42788 6

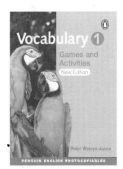

0 582 46566 4

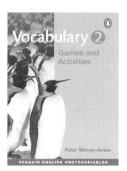

0 582 46565 6

0 14 081680 1

0 14 081659 3

0 14 081662 3

 www.penguinenglish.com